DOCUMENTING HISTORY

THE AMERICAN REVOLUTION

STEWART ROSS

FRANKLIN WATTS
A Division of Scholastic Inc.
NEW YORK TORONTO LONDON AUCKLAND SYDNEY
MEXICO CITY NEW DELHI HONG KONG
DANBURY, CONNECTICUT

First published by Evans Brothers Limited
2A Portman Mansions
Chiltern Street
London, W1M ILE

© Evans Brothers Limited 2001

First American edition 2001 by Franklin Watts
A Division of Scholastic Inc.
90 Sherman Turnpike
Danbury, CT 06816

Catalog details are available from the Library of Congress
Cataloging-in-Publication Data

ISBN 0-531-14613-8 (Lib. Bdg.)

Design – Neil Sayer
Editorial – Nicola Barber
Maps – Tim Smith
Consultant – Marianne S. Wokeck, Associate Professor,
Department of History, Indiana University, Indianapolis
Production – Jenny Mulvanny

Title page picture: Signing the Constitution

To find out more about the American Revolution, visit these
Web sites:

http://www.historyplace.com/unitedstates/revolution

http://www.pbs.org/ktca/liberty/chronicle/

http://earlyamerica.com/earlyamerica/milestones/

http://odur.let.rug.nl/~usa/D/#1776

ACKNOWLEDGMENTS

For permission to reproduce copyright pictorial material, the author and
publishers gratefully acknowledge the following:

cover: (background image) Peter Newark's American Pictures
(top left): Chateau de Versailles, France/Bridgeman Art Library
(top right): Peter Newark's American Pictures
(middle): Peter Newark's American Pictures
(bottom left): Peter Newark's American Pictures
(bottom right): Private Collection/Bridgeman Art Library
title page: (signing the Constitution) House of Representatives, Washington,
D.C./Bridgeman Art Library
page 7 (top) Peter Newark's American Pictures (bottom) Peter Newark's
American Pictures page 8 Private Collection/Bridgeman Art Library page 9
(left) Mary Evans Picture Library (right) Magdalen College, Oxford/Bridgeman
Art Library page 10 (top) Bridgeman Art Library (bottom) Bridgeman Art
Library page 13 Peter Newark's American Pictures page 14 Mary Evans
Picture Library page 15 (top) Peter Newark's American Pictures (middle) Peter
Newark's American Pictures page 16 Private Collection/Bridgeman Art Library
page 17 (top) Peter Newark's American Pictures (bottom) Philip Mould,
Historical Portraits Ltd, London/Bridgeman Art Library page 18 Peter Newark's
American Pictures page 19 Mary Evans Picture Library page 20 (top) Mary
Evans Picture Library (bottom) Peter Newark's American Pictures page 22
(top) Mary Evans Picture Library (bottom) Peter Newark's American Pictures
page 23 Mary Evans Picture Library page 24 Peter Newark's American
Pictures page 25 (top) Peter Newark's American Pictures (middle) Peter
Newark's American Pictures page 26 Peter Newark's American Pictures page
27 (top) Private Collection/Bridgeman Art Library (bottom) Peter Newark's
American Pictures page 28 (top) Peter Newark's American Pictures(bottom)
Private Collection/Bridgeman Art Library page 30 Peter Newark's American
Pictures page 31 (top) Peter Newark's American Pictures (bottom) Peter
Newark's American Pictures page 33 (left) Peter Newark's American Pictures
(right) Peter Newark's American Pictures page 34 (top) Mary Evans Picture
Library (bottom) Peter Newark's American Pictures page 35 Peter Newark's
American Pictures page 36 Chateau de Versailles, France/Bridgeman Art
Library page 37 Peter Newark's American Pictures page 38 (top) Peter
Newark's American Pictures (bottom) Christie's Images, London/Bridgeman
Art Library page 39 Bettmann/Corbis page 40 (left) Peter Newark's American
Pictures (right) Private Collection/Bridgeman Art Library page 41 Peter
Newark's American Pictures page 42 Peter Newark's American Pictures page

43 Peter Newark's American Pictures page 44 Peter Newark's American
Pictures page 45 Mary Evans Picture Library page 46 House of
Representatives, Washington, D.C./Bridgeman Art Library page 47 Peter
Newark's American Pictures page 48 (top) Peter Newark's American Pictures
(bottom) U.S. Library of Congress page 49 Peter Newark's American Pictures
page 50 (top) Private Collection/Bridgeman Art Library (bottom) Private
Collection/Bridgeman Art Library page 51 Peter Newark's American Pictures
page 52 New York Historical Society/Bridgeman Art Library page 53 Peter
Newark's American Pictures page 54 Mary Evans Picture Library page 55
(left) Yale University Art Gallery, New Haven, CT/Bridgeman Art Library (right)
Peter Newark's American Pictures page 56 (right) Bristol City Museum and Art
Gallery, UK/Bridgeman Art Library (bottom) Musée Carnavalet, Paris,
France/Roger-Viollet, Paris/Bridgeman Art Library page 57 British Library,
London/Bridgeman Art Library page 58 Peter Newark's American Pictures
page 59 (top) Peter Newark's American Pictures (bottom) Peter Newark's
American Pictures

For permission to reproduce copyright material for the documents, the author
and publishers gratefully acknowledge the following:

page 7 (bottom), page 33 From America Firsthand, Vol. 1 by Robert D. Marus
& David Burner, published by Bedford/St. Martins, 1998 page 13 (bottom),
page 53 From History of the United States of America by Hugh Brogan, published by Longman,1985 page 15 From Foundations of Colonial America: A
Documentary History by W. Keith Kavenagh, published by Chelsea House,
1973 page 19 From English Historical Documents, Vol. IX, ("American Colonial
Documents to 1776") edited by M. Jensen, published by Routledge, 1955
page 23, page 25 (top), page 29 (top), page 31 (top), page 45 (top), page
49 (bottom), page 59 (bottom): From Great Issues in American History: From
the Revolution to the Civil War, 1765-1865 by R. Hofstadter, published by
Vintage Books, an imprint of Random House, 1958 page 25: (bottom) From
The American Past by B. Wheeler, 1990 page 27, page 49 (bottom): From
An American History by Rebecca B. Gruver, published by Addison Wesley,
1976 page 35, page 39 From Treaties and Other International Acts of the
United States of America, Vol. 2, edited by Hunter Miller, published by the U.S.
Government Printing Office, 1931 page 43, page 45 (bottom): From Major
Problems in the Era of the American Revolution, 1760 – 1791 by Richard D.
Brown, published by DC Heath & Co, 1991 page 57 From Citizens by Simon
Schama, published by Viking Press, 1989

▰ CONTENTS ▰

LOOKING AT DOCUMENTS

The American Revolution brought the United States of America into being. In doing so, it changed the destiny of a continent. The events of the Revolution also set the groundwork for democratic movements throughout the world.

This book explains the complex nature of the American Revolution, how it began, and what its effects were. The first part examines the roots of the revolution, many stretching far back into British political life, and suggests that separation from Britain could not have happened without a previous revolution in thought. The middle section looks at the war itself, and the third part looks at how the principles of the Revolution were eventually enshrined in the Constitution. A short final section examines the impact of the Revolution on the United States and other parts of the world.

The American Revolution is based on close examination of documents written at the time. These include letters, speeches, newspaper articles, government papers, and comments by politicians, writers, soldiers, and ordinary people. To make the documents easier to read, they are printed in modern type. You will also find photographs of some of the original documents so you can see what they looked like. Any difficult or old-fashioned language is explained in the captions alongside the document itself.

A document's meaning and importance are not always obvious at first. As you read, ask yourself three important questions: when was it written, who wrote it, and why did they write it? The first question will help you figure out the context of a document. The second will help you understand the writer's point of view. Take a very simple word such as "people," for example. A modern reader understands this to mean everyone. But eighteenth-century society was dominated by adult white males. Without always realizing it, writers and speakers rarely used the term "people" to include children, nonwhites, and females. The third question will help you judge whether the writer is trying to offer unbiased facts, or whether he or she is arguing a case. Like a detective, you need to examine the evidence very carefully.

A NOTE ABOUT LANGUAGE
Most of the documents are printed using the words and phrases as they were first written. A few spellings have been modernized. Three dots (...) show where some of the original words have been left out. This has been done to make the documents easier to understand.

 The roots of the American Revolution lie in the English Revolution of the previous century. In this speech from 1647, an English soldier who had fought to overthrow King Charles I offers his view of fair government.

I really think that the poorest **he** that is in England hath a life to live, as the greatest he; and therefore truly... I think that every man that is to live under a government ought first by his own counsel put himself under that government.

What does this mean? Some words and phrases in the documents are difficult to understand. The captions alongside the documents give explanations of the highlighted areas of text. You can find out what this phrase means on page 11.

The ideas expressed in the opening sentence of the Declaration of Independence, written by Thomas Jefferson in 1776, are the principles of the entire American Revolution (see page 31).

We hold these truths to be self-evident, that all men are created equal, that they are endowed by their Creator with certain unalienable rights, that among these are life, liberty and the pursuit of happiness.

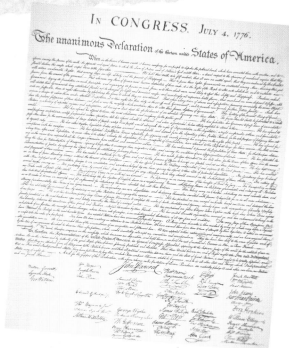

This excerpt from the diary of Albigence Waldo, a surgeon in Washington's army during the severe winter of 1777–8, helps us understand what army life was like (see page 33).

December 14... I am sick—discontented—and out of humor. Poor food—hard lodging—cold weather—fatigue—nasty clothes—nasty cookery—vomit half my time—smoked out my senses—the Devil's in it!

Jupiter Harmon, an African-American slave in Long Island, New York, published an "address" that showed his bitter disappointment that the freedom won by whites in the American Revolution had not been extended to African-Americans (see page 55).

That liberty is a great thing we may... judge so from the conduct of the white people in the late war. How much money has been spent and how many lives have been lost to defend their liberty? I must say that I have hoped that God would open their eyes, when they were so much engaged in liberty, to think of the state of the poor blacks, and to pity us.

CHAPTER 1

ORIGINS
THREE REVOLUTIONS IN ONE

The American Revolution was the process by which Britain's thirteen colonies in North America became a separate nation. The phrase "American Revolution" can be used to mean just the military conflict and the changes that occurred while it was in progress. According to this view, the Revolution began with the outbreak of fighting in 1775 and ended with the Peace of Paris in 1783.

An engraving of the Battle of Lexington (19 April 1775), the first battle of the American Revolution. Working more than 50 years after the event, the artist clearly wanted to present the British as the aggressors.

However, the American Revolution was more than just a military triumph. It reflected a revolution in thinking that started long before 1775. Nor was the Revolution over when the guns fell silent. It took the new country eight more years to establish a satisfactory form of government. Indeed, it was the Constitution (1787) and its Bill of Rights (1789) that changed a triumphant uprising into a true revolution.

The American Revolution was made up of three interwoven elements. First, there was a change in thinking, both in the colonies and in Britain, which gave rise to the opinion that people had a right to choose their

own form of government (self-determination). One logical conclusion drawn from these new ideas was that people also had the right to free themselves from a government not of their choosing. This part of the Revolution happened slowly and, in many cases, reluctantly. For example, when war broke out, it was initially viewed more as a civil war than a war of independence.

The second part of the Revolution was the war itself—the trial of strength that earned Americans their independence. The last part was the constitutional revolution. This cemented the new thinking and

the military victory in a form of government unlike any before it. Only when the Bill of Rights became law in 1791 was the American Revolution really over.

George Washington (1732–99) was the general who masterminded American victory in the Revolution.

REVOLUTION

Political revolution is a rapid, large-scale, and permanent political upheaval. The idea originated in ancient Greece. Greek philosophers Plato and Aristotle believed that revolutions were destructive because rapid change was bound to be poorly planned. Fear of revolution continued in medieval times, but during the Renaissance, attitudes changed. Thinkers such as English poet John Milton (above) and German philosopher Immanuel Kant suggested that revolution was progressive, allowing freedom to replace tyranny. This was the view of the majority of Americans who took up arms against the British crown.

 The war began on April 19, 1775. British troops going from Boston to Concord, Massachusetts, encountered armed resistance at Lexington. Fighting broke out. Later, the Massachusetts Assembly gave its account of what happened (right). Realizing how important it was to get public opinion on its side, Massachusetts blamed the British for starting the conflict.

Mustered means gathered together.

This means the British troops.

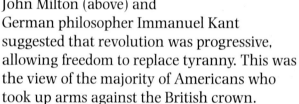

The town of Lexington... was alarmed, and a company of the inhabitants **mustered** on the occasion... the **regular troops** on their way to Concord marched into the said town of Lexington, and **the said company**, on their approach, began to disperse; notwithstanding this, the regulars rushed on with great violence, and first began hostilities by firing on said Lexington Company whereby they killed eight and wounded several others... the regulars continued to fire until those of the said company who were neither killed nor wounded had made their escape.

The Americans who had gathered.

THE ENGLISH REVOLUTION

The roots of the American Revolution reach back to the English Revolution in the seventeenth century. In 1600, political power in England rested with the monarch and Parliament. The king or queen and his or her chosen ministers made all important policy decisions. The monarch was also "supreme governor" of England's Protestant church, the Church of England.

The monarch was limited by a tradition that he or she could raise taxes only with the consent of Parliament. Parliament consisted of the House of Lords, made up of nobles and bishops of the Church of England, and the House of Commons. Members of the Commons (MPs) were elected from the towns and counties by the "political nation"—men of wealth

and standing. As monarchs were always short of money, they needed the support of the Commons to rule effectively.

The system worked reasonably well under James I (reigned 1603–25), as England's first American colonies were founded. But his son, Charles I (reigned 1625–49), alienated the political nation with a series of unreasonable policies. The two sides of government drifted farther apart and finally went to war. Parliament (mainly the House of Commons) won the English Civil War (1642–5), executed Charles I in 1649, and declared the country a republic.

The republic, led by Oliver Cromwell, failed to find a balance between the powers of Parliament and those of the head of the government. It also angered the political nation by

Oliver Cromwell (1599–1658)

abolishing the Church of England. In 1660, the old system of government was restored under Charles II. Nonetheless, the tension between monarch and parliament remained.

When Charles's Roman Catholic brother, James II

A contemporary painting of the execution of King Charles I in 1649. The event sent shock waves of horror throughout Europe and divided the American colonists.

(reigned 1685–8), tried to give the crown absolute power, the political nation deserted him. In the Glorious Revolution (1688–9), James's daughter Mary and her husband, William, accepted Parliament's invitation to become king and queen (Mary II and William III). James II fled to France.

The balance of power between the monarch and Parliament had now swung permanently in favor of Parliament. Parliament controlled taxes and expenditures. The monarch, though still nominally head of the government, had to appoint ministers with the approval of Parliament.

The English Revolution established the principle that the people—at least those with economic power—had the right to choose a government that acted in their interests. It was a principle that Americans would embrace in the next century.

THE CHURCH OF ENGLAND

King Henry VIII (reigned 1509–47) founded the Church of England when he renounced the authority of the pope and put himself at the head of the church. Henry's daughter, Queen Elizabeth I (reigned 1558–1603), re-established the church as a Protestant organization that retained aspects of Roman Catholicism. But many Protestants wished to "purify" the church of these remnants of Roman Catholicism. These opponents of the Church of England were known as Puritans. Some of them, dissatisfied with the religious state of affairs in England, emigrated to New England to establish what they hoped would be a more godly society.

After its victory in the English Civil War, the parliamentary army held a series of debates on how the country should be governed. The most radical contribution came from an ordinary soldier, Rainborough, who argued that everyone had a right to choose the government (right). His view was echoed by many Americans at the time of the Revolution.

> **He** means man.

> Here **as** means "just as."

Rainborough: I really think that the poorest **he** that is in England hath a life to live, **as** the greatest he; and therefore truly... I think that every man that is to live under a government ought first by his own **counsel** put himself under that government.

> **Counsel** means choice.

Since the political nation believed it had a right to be represented in Parliament, it could hardly argue that fellow countrymen living in America did not have that right. Here, English writer Soame Jenyns argues that Americans were indeed represented in Parliament.

> These were expanding industrial centers that had no MPs.

Many great names are quoted to prove that every Englishman, whether he has a right to vote for a representative or not, is still represented in the British Parliament... But then I will ask one question: Why does not this imaginary representation extend to America?... If the **towns of Manchester and Birmingham**, sending no representatives to parliament, are **notwithstanding** there represented, why are not the cities of Albany and Boston equally represented in that assembly? Are they not alike British subjects?...

> **Notwithstanding** means nevertheless.

THE THIRTEEN COLONIES

In 1497, John Cabot reached Newfoundland, Canada, and claimed North America for England. It took another 250 years for this claim to become a reality.

Spaniards established the first European settlement in North America at St. Augustine, Florida, in 1565. In 1608, France founded Quebec, Canada, and six years later Dutch fur traders built a trading post at Albany,

New York. Meanwhile, in 1607, the English had settled Jamestown, Virginia. After difficult beginnings, the colony prospered. By 1619, it had organized an assembly to discuss common problems. The principle of people having a say in their own government had moved from England to the "New World."

The New England colonies were born the following year, when the *Mayflower* pilgrims

settled at Plymouth. In 1691, Plymouth became part of another Puritan colony, Massachusetts (founded in 1630). By 1636, permanent settlements also existed in New Hampshire, Connecticut, and Rhode Island.

Maryland, founded in 1634, established another principle of colonial life when it passed an act of religious tolerance (1649).

In 1664, Delaware, New York, and New Jersey were added to England's growing North American empire, and in 1730, North and South Carolina (founded in 1653 and 1670) became individual colonies. Quakers settled in Pennsylvania in 1681, and James Oglethorpe founded Georgia, the last of the thirteen colonies, in 1733.

Around the English colonies stretched an arc of French settlements in Canada, on the shores of the Great Lakes, and along the Mississippi River valley. Their presence drew the English colonies together for protection. Not until the decisive French and Indian War (1754–63) was the French threat finally removed.

Two other important groups complete the picture of North America in the mid-eighteenth century. American Indians, largely driven from their lands in the east, still inhabited the vast unmapped territories of the West.

EUROPEAN SETTLEMENT OF NORTH AMERICA IN THE 17TH AND 18TH CENTURIES

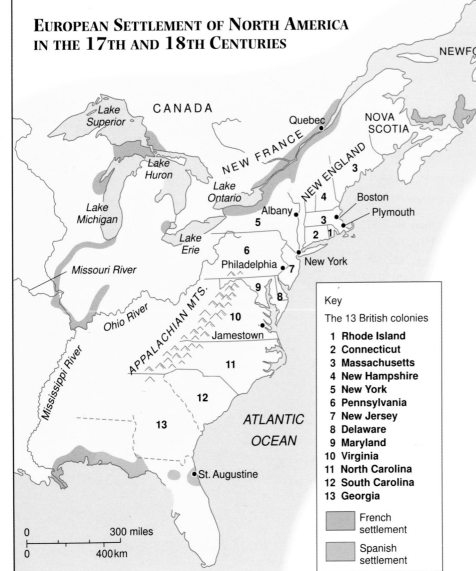

Key

The 13 British colonies

1 **Rhode Island**
2 **Connecticut**
3 **Massachusetts**
4 **New Hampshire**
5 **New York**
6 **Pennsylvania**
7 **New Jersey**
8 **Delaware**
9 **Maryland**
10 **Virginia**
11 **North Carolina**
12 **South Carolina**
13 **Georgia**

French settlement

Spanish settlement

0   300 miles
0   400km

The only interest they had in colonists' squabbles was when one side promised to leave them in peace. The second group were the black slaves brought from Africa since 1619. In 1770, there were about 500,000 slaves in British North America—about 20 percent of the total population. Questions of empire were largely irrelevant to them, unless white Americans were prepared to offer slaves the same freedoms they sought for themselves.

The Pilgrim Fathers were the English Puritans who sailed to the New World on the *Mayflower*. They landed in December 1620. This picture shows a romanticized view of their arrival. In reality, after weeks at sea, the thin and exhausted settlers would have been dressed in tattered clothes.

This description of the first sighting of Europeans by American Indians was written in the mid-eighteenth century. It refers to the arrival of English explorer Henry Hudson off Manhattan in 1609.

A long time ago, when there was no such thing known to the Indians as people with a white skin, some Indians who had been out fishing, and where the sea widens, espied at a great distance something remarkably large swimming, or floating on the water, and such as they had never seen before. They immediately returning to the shore, **appraised** their countrymen of what they had seen and pressed them to go out with them and discover what it might be. These together hurried out, and saw to their great surprise the phenomenon, but could not agree what it might be; some concluding it either to be an uncommon large fish, or other animal, while others were of the opinion it must be some very large house.

Appraised means told.

Inherent means fixed.

Speaking at the Stamp Act Congress of 1765, South Carolina delegate Christopher Gadsden put into words what had been going through American minds for some time. While referring to their English descent, he believed all colonists should now begin thinking of themselves as belonging to a single nation.

We should all endeavor to stand upon the broad and common ground of those natural and **inherent** rights that we all feel and know, as men and as descendants of Englishmen, we have a right to... There ought to be no New England men, no New Yorker, etc. known on the continent, but all of us Americans.

REVOLUTION IN MIND A "NEW WORLD"

The moment European settlers set foot on American soil, a distinctive American culture began to emerge. The first colonists were independent-minded and hardy. Once in America, separated from the "Old World" by 3,000 miles (5,000 kilometers) of ocean that took weeks to cross, they had no choice but to call on their own resources.

Life in the New World was extremely hard for early colonists. It is estimated that of about 14,000 immigrants to Virginia from 1607 on, all but 1,275 had died by 1624. In such conditions, rank, status, and wealth became almost irrelevant—colonists had to cooperate or perish. The qualities evident in those early years—independence, practicality, and a mistrust of tradition and inherited privilege—became part of the American character.

The instability of seventeenth-century English politics was another factor in the growth of a separate American identity. During the early years of the American colonies, the policies of different English governments toward the American colonists varied widely. As a result, Americans often directed their own development.

By the middle of the eighteenth century, other changes had increased the self-sufficiency and separateness of Britain's American empire. The colonists' population had grown from a few thousand in the early seventeenth century to about two million by 1760. They had extended their territory inland to between 150 and 200 miles (240 and 320 km) from the eastern coastline. Boston, with a population of 15,000, and Philadelphia, at 20,000, were among a handful of thriving cities. Where early colonists had struggled to grow enough crops to feed themselves and their families, a commercial economy based on cash crops and manufacturing was now expanding. For example, Virginian tobacco was widely exported, and shipbuilding flourished on the northeast coast. The establishment of the American Philosophical Society (founded in 1744) and several institutions of higher education, including Harvard (1636) and Yale (1701), showed that intellectual life was thriving.

Meanwhile, much political power had passed from British to American hands. In each colony, people voted for representatives to make up a legislative assembly. These assemblies passed laws on taxation, defense, and even the salaries of royal officials. However, all the colonies except five

Boston's busy harbor, in about 1750. The city was explored in 1614 and settled in the 1630s.

had royal governors. They were the monarch's representatives and, in theory, had widespread powers, such as making appointments and vetoing laws. The five colonies without royal governors—Massachusetts, Rhode Island, Connecticut, Pennsylvania, and Delaware—had always enjoyed considerable independence. In the remaining eight colonies, the governors' powers were limited by the need to work with local leaders. No governor could force his colony to do what he wanted.

Americans accepted their confusing relationship with Britain because, on the whole, the government in London interfered little in their day-to-day affairs. Furthermore, Americans and British had a common cause in resisting French incursions from the north and west. But when, after the successful but costly Seven Years War (1756–63), Britain attempted to tighten its grip, Americans began to think differently.

Harvard College, Cambridge, Massachusetts. By 1740, it was already establishing itself as an educational institution of high quality.

When asked by Britain to contribute to the fight against France in June 1754, delegates from seven colonies met in Albany, New York. Here Benjamin Franklin presented them with a "Plan of Union," featuring a "president general" and a representative "Grand Council." Although too ambitious for its time, it is an interesting preview of what was to come (below).

Benjamin Franklin (1706–90)

It is proposed that humble application be made for an act of Parliament of Great Britain, by virtue of which **one general government** may be formed in America...
1. That the said general government be administered by a President-General, to be appointed... by the crown; and a **Grand Council,** to be chosen by the representatives of the people of the several Colonies met in their respective assemblies...
9. That the assent of the President-General be **requisite** to all acts of the Grand Council, and that it be his office and duty to cause them to be **carried into execution**...
16. That ... the President-General, with the advice of the Grand Council have power to make laws, and lay and **levy** ... general duties, imposts, or taxes.

This means a federal government.

This was a sort of House of Representatives.

Levy means to raise.

Requisite means required.

This means carried out.

BRITAIN'S IMPERIAL TRIUMPH

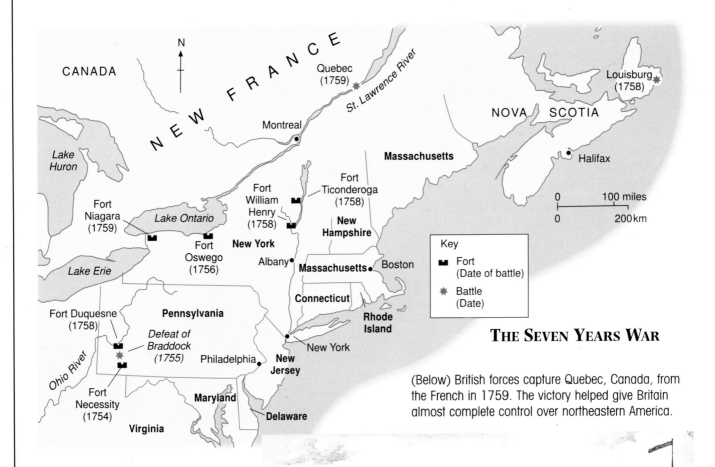

THE SEVEN YEARS WAR

(Below) British forces capture Quebec, Canada, from the French in 1759. The victory helped give Britain almost complete control over northeastern America.

A glance at the map on page 12 shows that in 1756 Britain was not the only colonial power in North America. Spain held Florida, while France controlled Canada and sought to extend its power south along the Ohio and Mississippi Rivers to New Orleans. While Spain's days of greatness were gone, both Britain and France dreamed of controlling the entire North American continent.

The issue was resolved by war. The conflict, known in America as the French and Indian War (1754–63) and in Europe as the Seven Years War (1756–63), was fought in both Europe and North America.

Britain's strategy, masterminded by Prime Minister William Pitt, was to have Britain's ally Prussia attack France, while Britain and its American colonial allies fought the French in North America.

The outcome was not guaranteed. Although outnumbered, France's forces in America were better organized, trained, and equipped than those of their enemies. They were also adept at forging alliances with

the American Indian population. In 1754, before the outbreak of war in Europe, colonial commander George Washington was driven from Fort Necessity (between Maryland and the Ohio River) by French forces. A year later, English general Edward Braddock suffered a devastating defeat at the Monongahela River. The French went on to capture Fort Oswego in 1756 and Fort William Henry in 1757.

In 1758, boosted by reinforcements from Europe, the British began to gain the upper hand. After failing to take Fort Ticonderoga, they seized Louisburg, Quebec (1759), and Montreal (1760), leaving Britain in control of eastern North America. This was confirmed in the Treaty of Paris (1763), by which the British gained Canada and all the land between the Mississippi River and the Atlantic coast.

Britain's triumph was a costly one, however. During the war, the national debt had almost doubled. The British commander in North America, General Jeffrey Amherst, estimated that the substantial garrisons (military posts) needed in North America to keep control over the newly acquired territories would cost over £300,000 a year. Where would the money come from? One obvious source was the colonies themselves.

TRAGEDY

Britain's victory was a disaster for the Ottawa, Huron, Chippewa, and other American Indian nations of the northeast. For a while, they had preserved a degree of independence by siding with France against Britain. Most had changed sides by 1759, lured by the promise that they would be left in peace after the war. When the promise proved false, Ottawa chief Pontiac launched a long and ultimately disastrous war (1763–6) to regain his territory.

Pontiac, the Ottawa chief who led the unsuccessful revolt against the British in 1763

In the 1680s, philosopher John Locke argued that the only valid government was one to which the people had given their consent. Later, this argument was used by Americans opposed to paying taxes levied by the British parliament.

English philosopher John Locke (1632–1704)

The **legislative** means parliament.

For example, laws authorizing the raising of taxes.

Americans had no representatives in the British parliament.

The constitution of the **legislative** is the first and fundamental act of society... by the consent and appointment of the people, without which no one man, or number of men, amongst them can have authority of **making laws**... that shall be binding to the rest. When any one, or more, shall take upon them to make laws whom **the people have not appointed so to do**, they make laws without authority, which the people are not therefore bound to obey.

PROCLAMATION AND PINE

THE PROCLAMATION OF 1763

N

CANADA

Great Lakes

St. Lawrence River

NOVA SCOTIA

Massa-chusetts

New Hampshire

Massachusetts

New York

Rhode Island

Penn-sylvania

Connecticut

New Jersey

Delaware

Ohio River

APPALACHIAN MTS.

Virginia

Maryland

North Carolina

ATLANTIC OCEAN

South Carolina

Georgia

West Florida
(British territory 1763–83)

East Florida

400 miles

600km

Key

(shaded)	The 13 colonies
(light)	Other British territory
(striped)	American Indian reserve
(white)	Spanish territory
——	Proclamation Line 1763

Many colonies had grievances against the British government, and therefore resented requests for financial assistance. The issue that caused the greatest irritation was Britain's attempt to regulate the colonies' western frontier. The Proclamation of 1763 limited the western territory into which the colonists could move. It also attempted to regulate trade between the colonists and American Indians. Royal officers known as commissioners were to supervise all trade beyond a line along the Appalachian Mountains.

Although the proclamation came too late to stop the Pontiac uprising, Britain saw it as a reasonable document. It wished to maintain peaceful relations with American Indians for largely financial relations—military confrontation was expensive. Britain also believed it had a moral duty to protect American Indians from the aggression of land-hungry colonists.

From the American point of view, however, the proclamation was unreasonable. By handing control of the West to the British crown, it reduced the power of colonial governments. It also

Bartering for furs. To the irritation of the British government, American colonists engaged in profitable trading with American Indians to the west of the Appalachian Mountains.

upset settlers who hoped to make their fortunes in the West. They condemned the proclamation as an oppressive measure imposed by an alien government.

Americans were also bothered by the existence of a British army in North America after the end of the French and Indian War. Britain said the army was needed to secure the western frontier, but colonists saw it as an insult to local forces. Moreover, like many Englishmen, they associated a standing (permanent) army with tyrannical government, such as the one in France.

The unwanted proclamation and standing army affected all the colonies. More local annoyances added to the feeling of discontent. For example, the Church of England had few supporters in New England. New Englanders, therefore, were angered when Archbishop of Canterbury Thomas Secker favored the Church of England over other Protestant churches, such as the Congregationalists. Secker banned Congregationalist missionary work among American Indians. Pennsylvania, New Jersey, and New York grumbled over the British government's power (abandoned in England long ago) to dismiss their judges when it wished. New Hampshire, Massachusetts, and Connecticut resented the White Pine Acts, which said that Royal Naval shipbuilders could use all white pine trees not growing on private property. And South Carolina was roused by a quarrel between its elected assembly and its dim-witted governor, who was appointed by the crown.

BISHOPS IN AMERICA

The wide range of Christian beliefs held by the settlers in America ensured that religious tolerance became a way of life in most colonies. Successive British archbishops recognized this and resisted the temptation to try and install Anglican bishops even in nominally Anglican colonies such as Virginia. Archbishop Secker opposed this policy. This fueled American mistrust of Britain's Anglican government, of which he was a part.

The insensitive behavior of Thomas Secker (1693–1768), Archbishop of Canterbury and head of the Anglican church, irritated New England Protestants at a time when Britain's colonial rule was attracting rising criticism.

 George III's Proclamation of 1763 showed concern for the welfare of American Indians.

Dominion means direct control.

This means all lands to the west of the Appalachian Mountains.

And whereas it is just and reasonable, and essential to our interest, and the security of our colonies, that the several nations or tribes of Indians with whom we are connected, and who live under our protection, should not be molested or disturbed... We do... declare it to be our royal will and pleasure... to reserve under our sovereignty, protection, and dominion, for the use of the said Indians, all the Lands and Territories not included within the limits of our said three new governments...

SEEDS OF REVOLUTION

George Grenville (1712–70), whose tax-raising measures led to a significant rise in tension between Britain and the American colonies.

British revenue officers deal with smugglers who are attempting to import goods into North America without paying a duty.

Britain's parliamentary system of government was more representative of the wealthier classes, who also paid the bulk of the taxes. Since the tax burden was higher than ever before, Prime Minister George Grenville decided to look for new sources of income.

The British had always seen their colonies as primarily commercial ventures. During the seventeenth century, parliament had passed several Navigation Acts to regulate and maximize profits from colonial trade. Colonial imports had to be carried in English- or colonial-built ships that were English-owned and operated. "Enumerated articles," such as tobacco, dyes, and sugar, that were shipped to or from the colonies had to pass through an English port or pay heavy duties. In America, English-controlled customs houses and law courts operated by the Royal Navy were responsible for enforcing the Acts.

During the French and Indian War, to stop illegal colonial trade with the French, Pitt instructed the Royal Navy to implement the Navigation Acts rigorously. Smugglers were hunted down and corrupt officials prosecuted. This harsh enforcement brought in extra revenue for Britain. So, although he knew it would be unpopular, Grenville maintained the Navigation Acts after the war. He also extended them, with a Sugar Act (1764) that reduced the duty on imported foreign molasses but imposed a high duty on refined sugar and banned the importing of foreign rum. The Currency Act (1764) banned colonial paper money because it was of little value compared to the British pound.

The Americans, accustomed to light taxation and minimal government, deeply resented Grenville's measures. Colonial businesses that had done well during the war, such as suppliers to the armed forces, struggled when peace was made. Grenville's legislation made things worse for them. It also raised serious questions of principle. At this stage very few Americans questioned Britain's right to control the colonies,

but many had serious worries about how that control was being exercised.

The British Admiralty Courts appeared to ignore the basic rights accorded to English citizens—the accused was presumed guilty instead of innocent, and cases were not heard by a jury. And Grenville's economic measures looked alarmingly like taxation disguised as trade regulation. In New England—particularly in Boston and Newport—community leaders stirred up resistance and planned a boycott of British goods.

A MATTER OF PRINCIPLE

Prime Minister George Grenville, an able but unimaginative administrator, believed that British MPs represented the colonies "virtually" (indirectly) in Parliament. He claimed this gave him the right to tax Americans with laws passed in London. Once Parliament had accepted this principle, the majority of MPs were too proud to back down. As Americans were equally convinced they were not represented in Parliament, virtually or otherwise, the stage was set for inevitable conflict.

The first Navigation Act was passed in 1651, less than two years after England had become a republic.
This section of the act insists that all English trade be carried in English ships.

This refers to the remaining members of the Long Parliament that first met in 1640.

This means colonies.

Commonwealth means community.

For the increase of shipping and the encouragement of the navigation of this nation... be it enacted by this **present Parliament**... that... no goods or commodities whatsoever of the growth, production or manufacture of Asia, Africa or America... as well of the **English plantations** as others, shall be imported or brought into this **Commonwealth** of England, or into Ireland, or any other lands... to this Commonwealth belonging... in any other ship or ships... whatsoever, but only in such as do truly and without fraud belong only to the people of this Commonwealth.

In a speech of 1761, Massachusetts lawyer James Otis (1725–83) challenged the British government's right to issue search warrants (writs of assistance) to enforce the Navigation Acts. He was one of the first Americans to base his resistance on the
principle of natural law. He says here that a law beyond human control gives everyone basic rights.

Arbitrary means unregulated.

Otis, like almost all Americans, regarded himself as English.

This means the natural law.

I take this opportunity to declare that whether under a fee or not... I will to my dying day oppose, with all the powers and faculties God has given me, all such instruments of slavery on the one hand and villainy on the other as this Writ of Assistance is... It appears to me the worst instrument of **arbitrary** power, the most destructive of **English liberty** and the fundamental **principles of law**, that ever was found in an English law-book.

NO TAXATION WITHOUT REPRESENTATION

Grenville figured that the Sugar Act and other measures would bring in about £45,000 ($165 million) a year. Since this amount was lower than the cost of maintaining the North American garrisons, he also introduced an American Stamp Duty Act.

"Stamp Duty" meant printing all legal and official papers, newspapers, pamphlets, and playing cards on paper carrying an embossed stamp. This paper could be bought only from stamp commissioners. It was manufactured in England, where a similar tax had proved efficient and easily collected.

Anno quinto

Georgii III. Regis.

C A P. XII.

An Act for granting and applying certain Stamp Duties, and other Duties, in the *British* Colonies and Plantations in *America*, towards further defraying the Expences of defending, protecting, and securing the same; and for amending such Parts of the several Acts of Parliament relating to the Trade and Revenues of the said Colonies and Plantations, as direct the Manner of determining and recovering the Penalties and Forfeitures therein mentioned.

An example of the type of stamp, embossed on British-made paper, which most legal and printed documents had to carry (above).

This (right) is the first page of the notorious Stamp Act, passed by the British parliament early in 1765.

The Stamp Act became law on March 22, 1765. Grenville's previous measures had doubled the tax Americans paid to Britain. The Stamp Act threatened to double it again. Because duty was payable on shipping documents, it struck where America was most sensitive—trade. Furthermore, it directly affected some influential people in colonial society: lawyers, merchants, and journalists.

The Stamp Act was Parliament's first attempt to tax the colonies directly rather than through trade regulation. It produced a ferocious storm of protest. Under the banner "No Taxation Without Representation," mobs took to the streets in Boston, New York, and other large towns. Distributors of stamps were forced to step down. While most legal business ground to a halt, the proposed boycott of British goods came closer to reality.

The Stamp Act was condemned in pamphlets, letters, newspapers, local meetings, and assemblies. On October 7, 1765, delegates from nine colonies met in New York to discuss the situation. This Stamp Act Congress denounced the act as a violation of their right to be taxed only through elected representatives. The resolutions of this congress were significant: for the first time, the colonies were speaking with one voice.

Most scholars have seen the opposition by so-called "patriots" to the Stamp Act as evidence that Americans were starting to think of themselves as a separate nation. However, many twentieth-century historians believe that these popular uprisings were aimed more at wealthy colonists than at the British. The patriot mobs attracted the most disadvantaged people in colonial society—unskilled workers, sailors, the unemployed, and African-Americans—who resented the prosperity of fellow colonists.

KING GEORGE III (REIGNED 1760–1815)

George III (right) tested the balance between royal and parliamentary power established by the Glorious Revolution (1688–9). He was narrow-minded and certain of his authority, and he tried to influence affairs more than was reasonable or prudent. His determination never to surrender to colonial demands persuaded many Americans that he was the principal cause of the mounting tensions.

Esteem means regard.

Although the Stamp Act crisis is sometimes said to mark the beginning of the American Revolution, the language adopted by the 1765 Congress in the preface to its Stamp Act Resolutions of October 19 is a model of propriety.

The members of this Congress, sincerely devoted, with the warmest sentiments of affection and duty to His Majesty's Person and Government... **esteem** it our indispensable duty to make the following declarations of our humble opinion...
That His Majesty's... subjects in these colonies, are entitled to all the... rights and liberties of his... subjects within the kingdom of Great-Britain.
That it is inseparably essential to the freedom of a people, and the undoubted right of Englishmen, that no taxes be imposed on them, but with their own consent... or by their representatives.
That the people of these colonies are not, and from their local circumstances cannot be, represented in the House of Commons in Great-Britain.

The House of Commons.

Erroneous means false.

Sympathy for the American cause was strong in many parts of British society. The colonists had no stronger supporter in opposing the Stamp Act than Prime Minister William Pitt, who had master-minded victory in the wars of 1754 to 1763.

I beg leave to tell the **House**... my opinion. It is that the Stamp Act be repealed absolutely... [for] it was founded on an **erroneous** principle. At the same time, let the sovereign authority of this country over the colonies be asserted in as strong terms as can be devised... that we may... exercise every power whatsoever—except that of taking money out of their pockets without their consent.

FIRST BLOOD

The trade boycott organized by the anti-Stamp Act movement alarmed British merchants. This anxiety spread to Parliament, where the situation was saved by a change of government. In July 1765, George III replaced Grenville with the Marquis of Rockingham. Under pressure from his supporters, Rockingham repealed the Stamp Act and reduced the duty on molasses. However, he also introduced a Declaratory Act stating that Parliament kept control over the colonies "in all cases whatsoever." In other words, Parliament insisted it had the right to tax the colonies however it wanted.

Most Americans ignored the Declaratory Act and greeted the repeal of the Stamp Act with great rejoicing. In 1766, a new British official, Charles Townshend, introduced the "Townshend Acts"—import duties on necessities such as lead, glass, paint, paper, and tea. The revenue from these taxes was earmarked for official salaries as well as defense. Other measures confirmed that writs of assistance were legal, established new anti-smuggling institutions, and created a secretary of state for the colonies (1768).

After a period of relative quiet, Philadelphia lawyer John Dickinson alerted colonists to the dangers of Townshend's measures. He objected to all revenue-raising taxation issuing from London. He also said that assemblies would be powerless if they lost the right to grant (or withhold) official salaries.

The protests started again. Sons of Liberty—radical and sometimes violent groups that had first appeared during the anti-Stamp Act demonstrations—harassed officials and coordinated resistance. Assemblies drafted petitions and circulated letters of complaint. A policy of "nonimportation"—refusing to import a variety of British goods—spread through the colonies. This brought women into the patriot movement. They banned tea-drinking in their households and took to their looms to make up for the lack of imported wool and linen cloth.

In 1768, following a serious riot, four regiments of British troops were stationed in Boston. Relations between the patriots and the soldiers were calm at first. Then, on March 5, 1770, a mob of unemployed workers began pelting a customs house guard with snowballs and oyster shells. In the confusion that followed, the soldiers opened fire. Five patriots, including the African-American Crispus Attucks, were killed. The Boston Massacre had given the American cause its first martyrs.

Riot becomes a massacre: this early American engraving of the Boston Massacre reflects the feeling that it was an act of ruthless suppression.

John Dickinson expressed his views (below) in lively articles entitled *Letters from a Farmer in Pennsylvania*. Widely circulated, they played a key role in uniting the colonies behind the patriot position. At this stage, however, independence from Britain remained a last resort.

John Dickinson (1732–1808), the pamphleteer who caught the spirit of the American people

Here then, my dear country men ROUSE yourselves, and behold the ruin hanging over your heads. If you ONCE admit, that Great Britain may lay duties upon her exportations to us, for the purpose of levying money on us only... the tragedy of American liberty is finished... If Great-Britain can order us to come to her for necessaries we want, and can order us to pay what taxes she pleases... we are as **abject** slaves as **France and Poland** can show in **wooden shoes, and with uncombed hair.**

Abject means defenseless.

Both countries were regarded as tyrannies.

Examples of obvious signs of poverty.

SAMUEL ADAMS (1722–1803)

Samuel Adams, a strict Calvinist, ex-tax collector, and member of the Massachusetts Assembly until 1774, was undoubtedly the most outspoken patriot leader of his time. He was at the forefront of opposition to the Stamp Act and the nonimportation movement. Nevertheless, he was a very conservative man and, until 1776, refused to accept independence as the remedy to America's problems.

Samuel Adams, organizer of the Boston Tea Party of 1773 (see page 27)

In the murder trial that followed the Boston Massacre, British commander Thomas Preston gave the following evidence. He was represented in court by patriot and future president John Adams, and was found innocent.

One of the soldiers having received a severe blow with a stick, stepped a little to one side and instantly fired... On this a general attack was made on the men by a great number of heavy clubs and snowballs... by which all our lives were in imminent danger... Instantly three or four of the soldiers fired... On my asking the soldiers why they fired without orders, they said they heard the word "fire" and supposed it came from me. This might be the case as many of the mob called out "Fire! Fire!" But I assured the men that I gave no such order, that my words were, "Don't fire! Stop your firing!"

OVER THE EDGE

On the day of the Boston Massacre, Britain's new prime minister, Lord North, announced that all the Townshend duties except those on tea were to be withdrawn. This announcement, in addition to a more relaxed policy on westward expansion, was seen as a colonial victory, and the nonimportation movement fizzled out.

However, the fundamental differences between Britain and its colonies remained, and patriots such as Samuel Adams remained deeply suspicious. Tensions mounted again in 1772, when Rhode Island smugglers burned the HMS *Gaspee*, an anti-smuggling patrol vessel. Rumors circulated that Britain planned to pay some colonial officials directly. This would reduce the power of colonial assemblies, who voted on official salaries and therefore had some control over office-holders. In response, a network of inter-colonial corresponding societies was established. Through them, colonial leaders kept in touch and coordinated opposition to unpopular government policies.

In 1773, Lord North introduced the Tea Act. This was an attempt to reduce smuggling by allowing the East India Company to sell duty-paid tea at a price below that charged by smugglers. The Sons of Liberty denounced this as a plot to ruin colonial merchants and seduce Americans into paying extra duties on their favorite drink. In December, Samuel Adams organized a band of Bostonians to dress as American Indians and dump some £10,000 ($15,000) worth of duty-paid tea into Boston harbor.

The exasperated British government responded with five laws (the "Intolerable Acts") that closed the port of Boston, altered the town's charter in favor of the governor, and strengthened direct royal government. In response, in September 1774, delegates from all the colonies except Georgia gathered in Philadelphia for a Continental Congress. They agreed to support an embargo of British goods, cutting trade with Britain. The more radical delegates talked of America becoming a separate state under the Crown and therefore not subject to Parliament. A few even spoke of independence.

Fearing a military response from Britain, a few colonial

This 1774 cartoon shows a tax collector (who has been tarred and feathered) being forced to drink British tea. In the background, the Stamp Act is pinned upside-down to a Liberty Tree.

leaders (mostly in Massachusetts) gathered weapons and organized volunteers into a militia (citizen army). The inevitable armed clash finally came on April 19, 1775. British troops went to investigate reports of an arms supply at Concord, Massachusetts. Alerted by Paul Revere, local militiamen skirmished with the British at Lexington Green, Concord, and along the Concord-Boston road. By nightfall, the British had suffered 273 casualties, and the Americans had lost 92 soldiers. The war had begun.

THE BOSTON TEA PARTY

Much of the East India Company tea that arrived in America in 1773 remained on board the ship or locked away in customs houses. But Governor Hutchinson of Massachusetts was determined to see the Boston consignment unloaded and sold. The result was the Boston Tea Party, when 342 tea chests were smashed open and their contents scattered on the water. The calculated gesture of defiance horrified moderate colonists. It prompted the Intolerable Acts and was an important step on the road to war.

The Boston Tea Party, 1773

Only recently has the significant contribution of American women to the revolutionary movement been recognized. Women made nonimportation possible by working to produce goods and materials that had previously been imported. Moreover, as this letter from a Philadelphia woman shows (below), many were as fervent as the menfolk in their determination not to submit to British "slavery."

An American stocking-maker. To support the revolution, American women manufactured goods that had previously been imported from Britain.

Most luxury goods were imported from Britain.

Actuates means drives.

Niccolo **Machiavelli** was an influential Italian political thinker at the time of the Renaissance.

I know this—that as free I can die but once, but as a slave I shall not be worthy of life. I have the pleasure to assure you that these are the sentiments of all my sister Americans. They have sacrificed assemblies, **parties of pleasure, tea drinking and finery,** to that great spirit of patriotism that **actuates** all degrees of people throughout this extensive continent... You say you are no politician. Oh sir, it requires no **Machiavellian head** to discover this tyranny and oppression. It is written with a sunbeam.

REVOLUTION IN FACT
TRAITORS

The first two stages of the American Revolution now began to merge. Although the process of cutting America's political ties with Britain had begun, the revolution in thinking was by no means complete. Most colonists still thought of themselves as British and hoped for a peaceful settlement with the king, if not with the parliament.

Meanwhile, the war continued. At this stage, the fighting was largely around Boston and along the frontier with Canada, which remained loyal to Britain. British forces in the port of Boston were besieged by militiamen from all over New England. Americans took Bunker Hill, from which they could bombard Boston. A major battle was fought on June 17, 1775, when the British lost one thousand men while recapturing

George Washington takes command of the army (1776).

Bunker Hill. The Americans had greater success on the Canadian front. Advancing slowly but steadily north, they captured Montreal in November.

Amid cries of "Liberty or Death," the Second Continental Congress gathered in May 1775. To preserve liberty, delegates took on the role of provisional government. Committees to handle finance and foreign affairs were established. Because the volunteer militia was no match for Britain's professional soldiers, Americans planned a professional force of their own—the Continental Army. George Washington, head of the militia in Virginia, was appointed commander in chief.

The delegates did not see themselves as traitors. Most of them still wanted a peaceful settlement with Britain. They drafted the Olive Branch Petition to George III, explaining that their problem was not with him but with his overbearing parliament. The next day, they justified their position in the "Declaration of the Causes and Necessity of Taking Up

Bunker Hill, outside Boston, July 1775

Arms." Then, while waiting to see what their king would reply, they made arrangements for the establishment of a navy, entered secret discussions with other nations for support, and encouraged the colonies to set up committees of public safety to direct military operations. Most royal governors had by now fled abroad.

The year ended on a somber note. George III rejected Congress's petition, declared America to be in a state of rebellion, and pronounced all Congressional delegates as traitors. Britain banned all trade with the colonies and hired twenty thousand German mercenaries (professional soldiers) to fight in the colonies. For Americans, "Liberty or Death" had become very real alternatives.

The "Declaration of the Causes and Necessity of Taking Up Arms" by Congress (right) includes this account (below) of how the fighting started.

General Gage... on the 19th day of April sent out... a large detachment of his army, who made an unprovoked assault on the inhabitants of... the town of Lexington... [They] murdered eight of the inhabitants and wounded many others. From thence the troops proceeded... to the town of Concord, where they set upon another party of the inhabitants of the same province, killing several and wounding more, until compelled to retreat by the country people suddenly assembled to repel this cruel aggression. Hostilities, thus commenced by the British troops, have been since prosecuted by them without regard to faith or reputation.

Some slaves responded with hope to the colonists' talk of rights and liberty. In this letter of April 20, 1773, to the Massachusetts Assembly, Peter Bestes and others point out that those who demand freedom for themselves should also be prepared to grant it to others.

Actuated means moved.

Your house means the assembly.

Sir, The efforts made by the legislative of this province... to free themselves from slavery, gave us, who are in that deplorable state, a high degree of satisfaction. We expect great things from men who have made such a noble stand against the designs of their fellow-men to enslave them... As the people of this province seem to be **actuated** by the principles of equity and justice, we cannot but expect **your house** will... take our deplorable case into serious consideration, and give us that ample relief which, as men, we have a natural right to.

COMMON SENSE

Thomas Paine, a recent immigrant from England, found a way to clearly express what the majority of Americans were thinking. His pamphlet *Common Sense* (January 1776) said that George III was a "Royal Brute," and God was the true "king" of America. The struggle, he said, was not about "a few vile acts," but about full independence; British "corruption" was poisoning the New World.

Few pieces of writing have had such an immediate impact. *Common Sense* was quoted from pulpits, discussed around campfires, and read in living rooms all over America. It reminded the colonists why they had embarked on their great undertaking and where they were headed. Its enthusiastic reception ended all hope of compromise with Britain.

The defiant mood spread from the provinces to the government in the Continental Congress. Orders went out to attack British ships, open American ports to merchants from other nations and, for the duration of the crisis, ban the import of slaves. The acceptance of Congress's authority was a crucial development toward nationhood. Locally, colonial assemblies that had not already done so were transforming themselves into states.

Meanwhile, influential voices in the states and Congress were echoing Paine's call for a formal justification of American military action. In June 1776, Congress established a committee to draw up the necessary document. Its five members were John Adams (Massachusetts), Benjamin Franklin (Pennsylvania), Roger Sherman (Connecticut), Robert R. Livingston (New York), and Thomas Jefferson (Virginia). They proved to be some of the wisest and sharpest minds ever assembled.

Congress revised the committee's document, written by Thomas Jefferson, and adopted it on July 4, 1776. This day is emblazoned in history as a landmark in the struggle for democracy. The first part of the Declaration of Independence, which justified rebellion against a government that denied natural rights, set out the principles upon which all subsequent democratic governments have been established. The ideas, many adapted from John

The five-man committee that drew up the Declaration of Independence offers its document to John Hancock, president of the Continental Congress, to inscribe the first signature.

Locke, were not new, but never before had they been expressed with such clarity.

The second part of the Declaration owed much to Paine's ideas. It listed Britain's crimes and laid them all at the feet of George III. Parliament was not mentioned. Jefferson knew that rebellion against a tyrant would attract far more sympathy than rebellion against an institution.

THOMAS PAINE (1737–1809)

Born in Norfolk, England, Thomas Paine worked as a corset-maker, sailor, schoolmaster, and tax collector. In 1774, he met Benjamin Franklin, who helped him emigrate to Philadelphia. Here, working as a radical journalist, he wrote *Common Sense*. He continued fighting for radical causes for the rest of his life. His atheism (denial of God's existence) eventually alienated most of his supporters, and he died in poverty on the farm that grateful New Yorkers had given him many years before.

Jefferson said that in writing the Declaration of Independence (below, right) he had tried to write "an expression of the American mind."

This means rights that cannot be removed.

We hold these truths to be self-evident, that all men are created equal, that they are endowed by their Creator with certain **unalienable rights**, that among these are life, liberty and the pursuit of happiness. That to secure these rights, governments are **instituted** among men, deriving their just powers from the consent of the governed. That whenever any form of government becomes destructive to these ends, it is the right of the people to alter or to abolish it, and to institute new government.

In CONGRESS. July 4. 1776.
The unanimous Declaration of the thirteen united States of America.

Instituted means set up.

The introduction to Thomas Paine's *Common Sense* cleverly lifts the American cause from the specific to the general, making it part of a universal struggle for the freedom of people everywhere.

This is an exaggeration—no colony had been so ravaged.

The cause of America is in a great measure the cause of all mankind. Many circumstances have, and will arise, which are not local, but universal, and through which the principles of all lovers of mankind are affected... The laying of a country **desolate with fire and sword**, declaring war against the natural rights of all mankind, and **extirpating** the defenders thereof from the face of the earth, is the concern of every man to whom nature hath given the power of feeling.

Extirpating means removing.

THE BUSINESS OF WAR

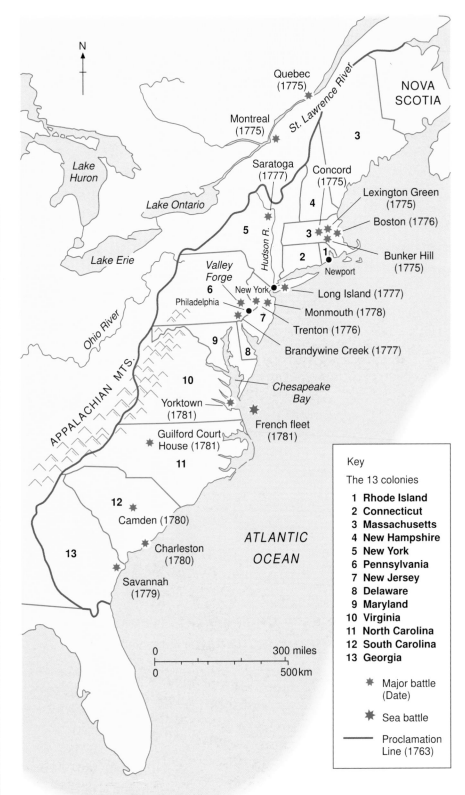

THE AMERICAN WAR OF INDEPENDENCE 1775–83

The Revolutionary War was at first waged by small, undisciplined armies led by inexperienced commanders. Although some 400,000 Americans enlisted in their local militia or the Continental Army, they generally served for only a few months. The total in arms at any one time never reached 30,000, and American commander George Washington could rely on no more than 5,000 regular soldiers. Britain's professional army, including many foreign mercenaries, was larger—but not large enough to subdue the Americans.

The British hung on to Boston until March 1776, when they evacuated the town. In June they suffered another setback at Charleston, South Carolina. They had better luck in the north, however, when the Americans failed to take Quebec and called off their invasion of Canada.

Meanwhile, a large British force, under the command of General William Howe and his brother Admiral Lord Richard Howe, landed on Long Island and drove General Washington from New York. After this defeat, it looked as if the American cause was lost. But Washington seized the initiative with a daring Christmas raid across the Delaware River that brought him a thousand prisoners and stirred his soldiers to stiffen their resolve.

The campaigns of the following year (1777) changed the course of the war. The British had planned to split the north from the

General Horatio Gates (1728?–1806) reviews the British prisoners that came into his hands after their surrender at Saratoga, October 1777.

THE COST OF WAR

Congress had serious problems paying for the war. Unable to levy taxes, it borrowed about $16 million, collected around $5.5 million from the states, and printed some $240 million in paper notes. These were not backed by gold or silver, and soon became almost worthless. Each state also printed its own (equally worthless) money. As soldiers in the Continental army were paid low wages in useless money, it was remarkable that the army held together at all.

Hardly worth the paper it was printed on: an American $20 bill of 1775

south and overcome each part in turn. General John Burgoyne advanced slowly from Canada to link up with Howe on the Hudson River. But Howe decided not to wait and moved off by sea to Pennsylvania. He defeated Washington at Brandywine Creek on September 11 and entered Philadelphia, the American capital at the time, two weeks later. However, it was now too late for Howe to get back to help Burgoyne, who had struggled

through to the Hudson. After defeats at the hands of American generals Benedict Arnold and Horatio Gates, Burgoyne surrendered at Saratoga on October 17. The victory raised hopes on both sides of the Atlantic, and the French, who had been secretly assisting the Americans since 1776, finally committed themselves to full-scale war with Britain.

Washington's army spent the severe winter of 1777–8 camped at Valley Forge, a commanding height on the road north from Philadelphia. The men endured terrible deprivation, as this excerpt from the colorful diary of army surgeon Albigence Waldo relates. Nevertheless, Washington used the time to discipline and train his recruits into an effective fighting force.

Fatigues means tiredness.

Alacrity means alertness.

December 14. The Army... now begins to grow sickly from the continued **fatigues** they have suffered this campaign. Yet they still show a spirit of **alacrity** and contentment not to be expected from so young troops. I am sick—discontented—and **out of humor**. Poor food—hard lodging—cold weather—fatigue—nasty clothes—nasty cookery—vomit half my time—smoked out my senses—the Devil's in it! I can't endure it! Why are we sent here to starve and freeze? What sweet **felicities** have I left at home! A charming wife—pretty children—good beds—good food—good cookery—all agreeable—all harmonious. Here all confusion...

Felicities are joys.

This means in a bad mood.

ALLIES

For a time, France helped the American rebels secretly—for example, France was America's chief source of gunpowder—rather than making a formal alliance. Not long before, France had been at war with the American colonists in the French and Indian War. Moreover, France itself was a colonial power and was hardly eager to promote rebellion in its own colonies.

Nevertheless, the prospect of avenging the humiliation of 1763 proved too tempting. Guided by the skillful diplomacy of Benjamin Franklin, representatives of the American and French governments signed pacts of alliance on February 6, 1778.

British prime minister Lord North had foreseen what might happen after Saratoga. In an effort to bring the war to a speedy conclusion before Britain's European enemies became involved, he proposed that America become a self-governing state within the British

The British warship *Royal William* in about 1757. Although the Royal Navy was powerful, during the Revolutionary War it was stretched beyond its capabilities.

empire. Americans might have accepted such an idea before the fighting broke out. But now they were an independent nation at war, and North's proposal fell on deaf ears.

The entry of France into the war added greatly to Britain's difficulties. The French attacked Britain's colonies in the Caribbean and elsewhere, and hindered its shipping in the Atlantic. The appearance of a powerful French fleet in American waters stretched the British Royal Navy to its limits. Spain joined the anti-British coalition in July 1779, and the United Provinces (the Netherlands) joined in December 1780. Russia, Sweden, and Denmark formed an Armed Neutrality (1780), pledging to use force to stop the Royal Navy from interfering with their trade with its enemies. As a result, Britain lost control of the seas for the first time in that century.

France seized the Mediterranean island of Minorca, besieged Gibraltar, and took a number of Caribbean islands. At one point, France and Spain contemplated a joint invasion of Britain itself. In such circumstances, it became even more difficult for Britain to reinforce and supply its forces in America.

If Britain was going to win the

The Battle of Monmouth Court House, in which Washington's army showed a newfound discipline

war, a decisive victory early in 1778 was essential. General Howe missed this opportunity when he failed to strike at Washington's weakened army at Valley Forge in Pennsylvania. In May, General Henry Clinton replaced Howe and left for New York. Washington's army, rested, reinforced, and reorganized, attacked Clinton at Monmouth Court House, New Jersey, on June 28. Although neither side had a clear victory, the American soldiers displayed a new discipline and courage. The British, with no hope of victory in the north, turned their attentions to the colonies in the south.

THE FIRST AMERICAN DIPLOMATS

The spy-story antics (such as writing in invisible ink) of Congress's first emissaries to France, Silas Deane and Arthur Lee, made America's diplomatic efforts look foolish at first. In December 1776, this situation was transformed by the arrival of world-famous scientist Benjamin Franklin. He used his familiarity with European society to win French hearts by acting the part of an unsophisticated pioneer. His charm and diplomacy helped forge the Franco-American alliance, and he remained the American minister in Paris until 1785.

A meeting of two worlds: Benjamin Franklin is presented to the king of France, 1776.

The Franco-American alliance of February 1778 (right) was set up to protect the United States. However, both parties knew that France would use the war to attack British colonies elsewhere.

France did not officially declare war on Britain until later in the year.

ARTICLE 2
The essential and direct end of the present defensive alliance is to maintain effectually the liberty, sovereignty, and independence absolute and unlimited of the said United States, as well in matters of government as of commerce.

Captain Alexander Graydon, remembering the problems he had recruiting men for his company in 1776, dispels the idea that all Americans were ready to fight for "Liberty or Death."

Enlist means to join the army.

A number of fellows at the tavern [in Frankford]... indicated a desire to enlist, but although they drank freely of our liquor, they still held off. I soon perceived that the object was to amuse themselves at our expense... One fellow... began to grow insolent... At length the... ruffian... squared himself for battle and advanced towards me... Taking excellent aim, I struck him with the utmost force between the eyes and sent him staggering to the other end of the room... This incident would be little worthy of relating, did it not serve in some degree to correct the error of those who seem to conceive the year 1776 to have been a season of almost universal patriotic enthusiasm.

YORKTOWN

It took a while for the full impact of the French alliance to be felt. In the meantime, American commanders continued to suffer from the problems that had plagued them all along—desertions, defections, and mutinies resulting from poor provisions, confused terms of enlistment (soldiers were not sure how long they were expected to serve), and low pay.

In these circumstances, it looked as if the British campaign to overcome the southern colonies might succeed. While Clinton remained at his base in New York, in autumn 1778, General Archibald Campbell carried out a successful seaborne invasion of Georgia, took Savannah, and soon controlled the whole state.

Clinton himself then took command and, on May 12, 1780, captured Charleston, the most important city in the South. About five thousand American soldiers, including three generals, were captured. Then, fearing a French attack on Newport, Rhode Island, Clinton returned to New York. He left eight thousand men in Charleston under the command of General Charles Cornwallis.

Buoyed by recent success, Cornwallis struck north and, in August, smashed the army of General Gates at Camden, South Carolina. Advancing into North Carolina, at Guilford Court House he met stiffer resistance from new American commander Nathaniel Greene before moving on to Virginia. Here Cornwallis began building up a base at Yorktown, where he expected to be supplied from the sea. Meanwhile, Americans had recovered their position in South Carolina and contained the remaining British forces in Charleston and Savannah.

By late summer, Cornwallis's position was deteriorating fast. While American forces prevented

A French artist's impression of American and French generals cooperating during the siege of Yorktown, 1781

his moving inland, a large French fleet carrying three thousand troops under the command of the Count de Grasse was sailing up from the West Indies to join the siege. In September, Washington moved south from New York. The fate of Cornwallis was sealed when de Grasse overcame the local British fleet in Chesapeake Bay on September 5. Washington arrived at Yorktown three weeks later. On October 19, Cornwallis surrendered his entire army of seven thousand men. As they handed over their weapons, the band reportedly played "The World Turned Upside Down."

The French naval victory off Chesapeake Bay in September 1781 ended any hope that the British garrison in Yorktown could be relieved.

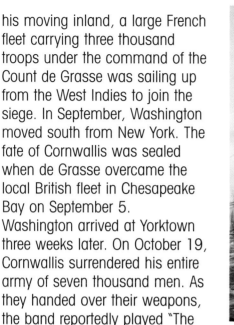 **British grenadier Lieutenant Hale, describing the British advance before Monmouth Court House, gives some insight into the terrible conditions endured by eighteenth-century soldiers.**

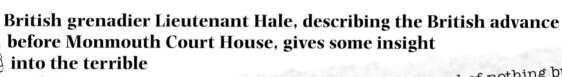

We proceeded five miles in a road composed of nothing but sand which scorched through our shoes with intolerable heat; the sun beating on our heads with a force scarcely to be conceived in Europe, and not a drop of water to assuage our parching thirst. A number of soldiers were unable to support the fatigue, and died on the spot. A corporal who had by some means procured water, drank to such excess as to burst and expired in the utmost torments. Two became raving mad, and the whole road, strewed with miserable wretches wishing for death, exhibited the most shocking scene I ever saw.

Procured means found.

Expired means died.

 The Articles of Capitulation accepted by Cornwallis at Yorktown specify precisely how the surrender was to be conducted.

This means Yorktown.

This means flags rolled up.

Article III... The garrison of York will march out to a place to be appointed in front of the posts, at two o'clock precisely, with shouldered arms, colors cased, and drums beating a British or German march. They are then to ground their arms, and return to their encampments, where they will remain until they are despatched to the places of their destination.

PEACE AND RECOGNITION

"Oh God! It is all over!" groaned British prime minister Lord North when he heard of the surrender at Yorktown. It was one of the few times during the war when he evaluated the situation correctly, and a few months later he resigned.

The war in America was now over. The new British government opened peace talks with the United States in 1782. While these were going on, thousands of American loyalists who had supported the British cause, as well as most British forces, were evacuated.

The negotiations, conducted on behalf of Congress by Benjamin Franklin, John Adams, and John Jay, were long and complicated because they also involved France, Spain, and Holland. At first, the Americans worked with France. In time, however, they realized that while

Hail the victor! General George Washington enters New York in November 1783. Military success had made Washington famous throughout North America and most of Europe.

the French accepted American independence, they were secretly trying to ensure that the United States would be a weak nation, possessing territory only to the east of the Appalachian Mountains. The Americans responded by entering secret negotiations of their own. These resulted in a treaty with Britain in 1782, which was confirmed by the wider peace signed at Paris

British warships launch a successful attack on two French frigates in April 1782. Late in the war, British naval successes restored some of the Royal Navy's battered prestige.

the following year.

Congress did not gain control over Canada as it had wanted, but Britain agreed to most of its other demands. First, the independence of the states was accepted. The new country was given all territory between the Atlantic Ocean and the Mississippi River, and between the Great Lakes and Florida. Britain also agreed to give American citizens fishing rights off Newfoundland.

The Treaty of Paris underscored a remarkable achievement—the establishment of the United States of America as an independent republic. But tricky questions remained. Just how united were the states? And what was their relationship with Congress? Only when these questions were answered would the American Revolution be complete.

WOMEN AT WAR

Many thousands of American women played a vital role in the war effort. Some gave money and goods. Others helped in more practical ways, gathering and passing on information, tending the sick and wounded, and sending provisions. Deborah Samson, a nineteen-year-old schoolteacher, disguised herself as a man and served in the Continental Army for three years. Mercy Otis Warren wrote a number of propaganda plays, of which *The Group* (1775) was most popular. Although not performed, these plays were widely printed in newspapers, signed with a pseudonym because it was not considered respectable for a woman to write. Warren also wrote poetry. Below is an excerpt from her poem "Political Reverie, 1776":

Mercy Otis Warren (1728–1814)

No despot here shall rule with awful sway,
Nor orphan's spoils become the minion's prey;
No more the widow'd bleeding bosom mourns,
Nor injured cities weep their slaughter'd sons;
For then each tyrant, by the hand of fate,
And standing troops, the bane of every state,
For ever spurn'd, shall be removed as far
As bright Hesperus from the polar star;
Freedom and virtue shall united reign,
And stretch their empire o'er the wide domain...

The first article of the Treaty of Paris speaks of the independence of twelve separate states (Delaware was regarded as part of Pennsylvania) rather than a single nation.

His Brittanic Majesty acknowledges the said United States, viz., New Hampshire, Massachusetts Bay, Rhode Island and Providence Plantations, Connecticut, New York, New Jersey, Pennsylvania, Maryland, Virginia, North Carolina, South Carolina and Georgia, to be free sovereign and independent states, that he treats with them as such, and for himself, his heirs, and successors, **relinquishes** all claims to the government, **propriety**, and territorial rights of the same and every part thereof.

Relinquishes means surrenders.

Propriety means ownership.

ARTICLE I.
His Britannick Majesty acknowledges the said United States, viz. New Hampshire, Massachusetts Bay, Rhode Island and Providence Plantations, Connecticut, New York, New Jersey, Pennsylvania, Delaware, Maryland, Virginia, North Carolina, South Carolina, and Georgia, to be free, sovereign, and independent States, that he treats with them as such, and for himself, his Heirs, and Successors, relinquishes all Claims to the Government, Propriety, and territorial Rights of the same, and every Part thereof.

II.
And that all Disputes which might arise in future on the Subject of the Boundaries of the said United States may be prevented, it is hereby agreed and declared, that the following are and shall be their Boundaries, viz. From the North West Angle of Nova Scotia, viz. that Angle which is formed by a Line drawn due North from the Source of St. Croix River to the Highlands, along the said Highlands, which divide those Rivers that empty themselves into the River St. Lawrence from those which fall into the Atlantick Ocean, to the North Westernmost Head of Connecticut River; thence down along the

The Constitutional Revolution
Not Yet a Nation

The war had been won by thirteen American colonies acting together. In the process, they became independent states combined in a loose federation known as the United States. The common (federal) government of these states was the Continental Congress. Each of the thirteen states still had its own constitution and executive branch, legislature, and legal system.

The change from colony to state was made by adopting a written constitution. The states did this in different ways. Massachusetts followed the most democratic path by insisting that its constitution (1780) be adopted by popular vote. No two constitutions were the same, though they shared certain characteristics. They were broadly based on colonial charters and included a bill, or declaration, of rights. The power of the executive (governor)

was strictly limited—Pennsylvania had no governor at all. The right to vote was granted only to adult white males. In spite of the talk of rights and liberty, slavery remained, although the slave trade was still legal only in Georgia and South Carolina.

Nevertheless, the unity of the states during the war had planted a fertile seed in people's minds. The key document of the period—the Declaration of Independence—had been issued in the name of one "people," not thirteen states. Certain individuals—Thomas Jefferson, Benjamin Franklin, and George Washington—were the heroes not of a single state but of the United States. The word "American," rather than "Virginian," "New Yorker," or "New Englander," was increasingly used at home and abroad. And, after June 1777, there was a flag—the thirteen stars and stripes—that

STARS AND STRIPES

The first all-American flag, the Grand Union or Continental flag, was unfurled on January 1, 1776. Its use of the crosses of St. George and St. Andrew was felt to be too British, however, and Betsy Ross of Philadelphia was asked to design a new one. Her "stars and stripes" version, adopted in the summer of 1777, became a colorful and powerful symbol of unity.

Betsy Ross at home with her famous creation

The stars and stripes flag

symbolized the unity of the states as one country. An American nation was gradually emerging.

To the disappointment of African-Americans, the Revolution brought no change in the status of the nation's slaves, such as these tobacco plantation workers.

Pennsylvania's Act for the Gradual Abolition of Slavery, passed on March 1, 1780, shows that Americans could not easily justify the existence of slavery in a society fighting for liberty and justice. Even so, they did not abolish slavery immediately.

Abhorrence means hatred.

Were exerted means tried.

Thraldom means slavery.

When we contemplate our **abhorrence** of that condition to which the arms and tyranny of Great Britain **were exerted** to reduce us; when we look back on the variety of dangers to which we have been exposed, and how miraculously our wants in many instances have been supplied... we conceive that it is our duty... to extend a portion of that freedom to others... and a release from that state of **thraldom** to which we ourselves were tyrannically doomed, and from which we have now every prospect of being delivered.

Virginia prefaced its constitution (1776) with a Declaration of Rights. Its intention was to protect the rights of all people, but since many Virginians regarded slaves as "property," they retained this right to "ownership."

Compact means agreement.

This means to take from their heirs and successors.

Clause I. That all men are by nature equally free and independent, and have certain inherent rights, of which, when they enter into a state of society, they cannot, by any **compact**, **deprive or divest their posterity**; namely, the enjoyment of life and liberty, with the means of acquiring and possessing property, and pursuing and obtaining happiness and safety.

CONFEDERATION

The Articles of Confederation, finally accepted by all the states in 1781, gave Congress authority to conduct the foreign affairs of the states, establish a national postal service, regulate a federal bank, and oversee relations with American Indians. It also claimed all territory between the Appalachian Mountains and the Mississippi River on the states' behalf.

In reality, Congress had very little power. For example, it could not regulate trade, interfere in a state's internal affairs, or raise its own taxes. Each state had one vote in Congress; the votes of nine states were needed to collect Confederate funds. Even then, the states raised only one quarter of the money sought.

The Confederation's government had no permanent headquarters and gave no single person decision- or policy-making powers. Nor did it have a legal system to uphold or change its laws. To make matters worse, delegates sat for only one year at a time. As a result, Congress lacked continuity and experience.

It was soon clear that the Articles of Confederation were inadequate as a means of governing the new nation. The "half-starved, limping government," in the words of George Washington, ran into difficulties with Britain over treaty violations and with Spain (which had not been party to the 1783 peace settlement) over disputed lands in the Southwest. When the Confederate government appeared insensitive to their needs, people in Vermont considered becoming part of Canada, and settlers in what are now Kentucky and Tennessee threatened to declare independence.

The war had left the United States with a foreign debt of almost $8 million. Domestic debts were even higher. The U.S. currency was virtually worthless, and for a time only Spanish coins were accepted. British tariffs made exports to Britain and its empire prohibitive, and the imbalance of trade drained the new country of much of its gold and silver. State currencies also collapsed; taxes rose; and many businesses were badly hit by the fall in exports. Farmers suffered most of all.

In 1786, war veteran Captain Daniel Shays led a rebellion in Massachusetts. When Congress could not meet the state's request for help, it was clear that the Articles of Confederation had

A traveler leads his pack horse through a pass in the Appalachian Mountains toward the Great Plains.

failed. If the young republic was to survive, either the Articles had to be radically amended or an entirely new constitution had to be drafted.

Shays's Rebellion of 1786 finally persuaded many people that a new constitution was needed if the nation was to survive.

1785 LAND ORDINANCE

The Land Ordinance passed by Congress in 1785 was one of its most successful pieces of legislation. It planned how the territories of the northwest, for which Congress was responsible, were to be surveyed and sold. The land was divided into square townships, each of 36 square miles (93 square km). These were sold in 640-acre (1-square mile) sections at a price set by Congress. In each township, one section was reserved for a school.

The Articles of Confederation were more a "league of friendship" between independent states than a constitution for the United States. This is clear from Articles II and III (right). The states' authority over taxation is set out in Article VIII.

Article II. Each state retains its sovereignty, freedom and independence, and every power, jurisdiction and right, which is not by this confederation expressly delegated to the United States...

Article III. The said states hereby... enter into a firm league of friendship with each other, for their common defense, the security of their liberties, and their mutual and general welfare...

Article VIII. All charges of war, and all other expenses that shall be incurred for the common defense or general welfare, and allowed by the United States in Congress assembled, shall be defrayed out of a common treasury, which shall be supplied by the several states... The taxes for paying that proportion shall be... levied by the authority and direction of the legislatures of the several states...

This collection of Revolutionary documents, printed in London in 1785, includes the Articles of Confederation.

Defrayed means met.

These taxes were paid by each state.

Levied means raised.

PHILADELPHIA

In 1780, Alexander Hamilton, former secretary to George Washington and member of the Continental Congress, called for a convention to discuss strengthening the Articles of Confederation. His plea fell on deaf ears. Later, groups of states began meeting together to talk over their differences. The idea of a convention became more popular when representatives of Virginia and Maryland met in 1785 to discuss navigation on the Potomac River. The following year, five states sent delegates to a convention in Annapolis, Maryland, to discuss improving American commerce. Guided by Hamilton and James Madison, they concluded that the Articles of Confederation had to be redrafted. A report to this effect went out to the states.

The report arrived at about the same time as news of Shays's Rebellion. Alarmed, all the states except Rhode Island chose delegates to meet at the proposed convention in Philadelphia. Congress gave its blessing, and on May 14, 1787, the convention formally opened.

Most of the fifty-five delegates at the convention were young and wealthy and had played an active part in the war. They were also very talented. The leading figures included George Washington (elected president of the convention), Hamilton, Madison, Roger Sherman of Connecticut, Edmund Randolph (governor of Virginia), Rufus King of Massachusetts, John Dickinson, James Wilson, and the now elderly statesman Benjamin Franklin. The talks were held in secret.

The delegates worked on four main principles. First, the central government needed to be strengthened to give it direct powers over all citizens. Second, the rights of individual states must be protected. Third, rather than the whole electorate voting on every new law and proposal, government would consist of the people's elected representatives. Fourth, the legislative, executive, and judicial branches of government were to be kept separate. To achieve these aims, delegates soon agreed to abandon the Articles of Confederation and replace them with a brand new Constitution for the United States of America.

The State House in Philadelphia, where the Constitutional Convention met in 1787

"THE FATHER OF THE CONSTITUTION"
Virginia lawyer James Madison (1751–1836) graduated from Princeton in 1771 and, five years later, helped write Virginia's constitution. While serving in the Continental Congress, he became convinced of the inadequacies of the Articles of Confederation and tried to have them replaced. For his central role in the Constitutional Convention of 1787, he is traditionally known as the "Father of the Constitution." Under the new government he held various offices, including that of president (1809–17).

James Madison had perhaps the sharpest mind on the committee that drafted the 1787 Constitution.

The hottest topic of debate in the 1787 convention was how many delegates (or votes) each state should have in a new Congress. William Paterson of New Jersey was upset by Virginia's proposal to distribute power according to a state's population.

Give the large states an influence in proportion to their magnitude, and what would be the consequences? Their ambition will be proportionately increased, and the small states will have everything to fear.

The report of the delegates attending the Annapolis Convention included a call for a separate convention to examine the whole confederate structure of government (right).

This means to get the agreement.

Induced means led.

This means so broad.

[We] have been **induced** to think that the power of regulating trade is of **such comprehensive extent,** and will enter so far into the general system of the federal government, that to **give it efficacy**... may require a correspondent adjustment of other parts of the federal system...
Under this impression, [we]... beg leave to suggest... that it may essentially tend to advance the interests of the union if the states... would... use their endeavors to **procure the concurrence** of the other states in the appointment of **commissioners,** to meet at Philadelphia on the second Monday in **May next,** to take... such further provisions as shall appear to them necessary to render the constitution of the Federal Government adequate to the **exigencies** of the Union.

This means make it work.

Commissioners were delegates.

May next was May 1787.

Exigencies means needs.

"We, the People"

The 1787 Constitution was the crowning glory of the American Revolution. It confirmed the United States as a single nation and established a lasting framework for its government. Unique for its time, it has since served as a model for many other written constitutions around the world.

It took almost four months of debate to produce the finished document, and at times disagreement threatened to destroy the whole process. At first things went smoothly. It was agreed that the executive branch would be headed by an elected president. A supreme court would head the federal judiciary (court system). The legislature would have two parts, the House of Representatives and the Senate. The three branches of government would be separate, and the powers given to one branch would be balanced by checks (controls) given to another.

In June, the early agreement evaporated. The so-called Virginia Plan suggested that representation in the legislature be proportional to the population of each state. The smaller states feared they would be swamped by the "big four" (Virginia, Pennsylvania, New York, and Massachusetts), and called for equal representation for each state. Finally, a compromise suggested by Roger Sherman of Connecticut was accepted: one chamber (the House of Representatives) would be proportional to population; in the other (the Senate), each state would be represented equally.

Three further problems remained: slavery, the control of U.S. trade, and a bill containing a guarantee of individual rights. The first two issues were settled by compromise, but the finished Constitution contained no bill of

The signing of the Constitution

rights.

All but three delegates signed the new Constitution on September 17, 1787. The delegates then returned home to begin persuading their states to ratify (give their formal approval to) the Constitution as the supreme law of the land.

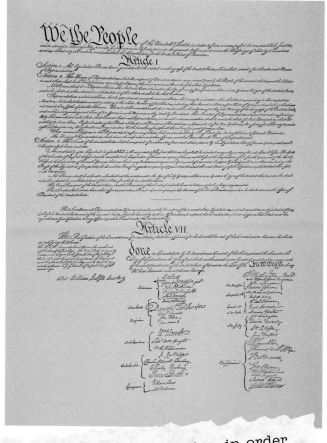

The opening words of the Constitution (right) state its purpose and explain that its authority comes neither from the states nor from the convention but directly from the people themselves.

We, the people of the United States, in order to form a more perfect Union, establish justice, insure domestic tranquillity, provide for the common defense, promote the general welfare, and secure the blessings of liberty to ourselves and our posterity, do ordain and establish this Constitution for the United States of America.

Article 1, Section 3, contains the "three-fifths compromise," which confirmed slavery as an integral part of the culture of the early republic. Here, "all other persons" means slaves, each counted as three-fifths of a person.

Apportioned means handed out.

Representatives and direct taxes shall be **apportioned** among the several States which may be included within this Union, according to their respective numbers, which shall be determined by adding the whole number of free persons, including those bound to service for a term of years, and excluding Indians not taxed, three-fifths of all other persons... The number of Representatives shall not exceed one for every thirty thousand, but each State shall have at least one Representative.

RATIFICATION

The authors of the Constitution determined that the document would take effect when ratified (accepted) by at least nine states. Each state's opinion was to be decided by a convention. This contradicted the Articles of Confederation, which stated they could be altered only by a unanimous vote of all the states. The new Constitution's authors got around the rule of the Articles by saying their plan did not alter the Articles, but rather replaced them by popular consent.

Many people who opposed ratification, known as Antifederalists, were suspicious of these arrangements. They mistrusted the delegates who had written the Constitution. In particular, many Westerners were wary of the manner in which a group of wealthy intellectuals had drawn it up in secret. Antifederalists were concerned that a powerful presidency might turn into a new

Once the restriction on westward expansion had been removed, American pioneers began pouring across the Appalachian Mountains to settle the rich farmlands beyond.

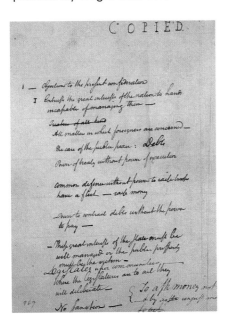

A page from Alexander Hamilton's notes, made for a vital speech given at the Constitutional Convention in 1787

monarchy. Others feared that federal institutions would overwhelm the states and ruin local economies. The absence of a bill of rights to protect individuals was another cause of concern.

Aware of the opposition, the pro-Constitution Federalists launched an extensive propaganda campaign. Washington and Franklin supported the campaign, but the major contribution came in the form of eighty-five essays

(collectively known as *The Federalist Papers*) written by Hamilton, Madison, and John Jay under the pseudonym "Publius" ("In the name of the people").

Delaware was first to accept the Constitution at its convention on December 7, 1787, followed by Pennsylvania five days later. New Jersey's acceptance came before Christmas, then Georgia's on January 2. A week later, Connecticut brought the number of ratifying states to five. When a bill of rights was proposed as a constitutional amendment, Massachusetts, Maryland, South Carolina, and New Hampshire raised the total to nine.

Although the required majority had been reached, New York and Virginia, with their wealthy and large populations, were crucial to the new republic. The battle to get them on board was long and hard. Finally, in late June, the Federalists triumphed at Virginia's convention with a vote of 89-79, and at New York's with a 30-27 vote. North Carolina joined in November, and Rhode Island in May 1790.

THE FEDERALIST PAPERS

The Federalist Papers appeared as a series of articles in New York newspapers. Although written to support the Federalist cause and urge New Yorkers to ratify the new Constitution, they went much further. The authors—Hamilton, Madison, and Jay—discussed a wide range of political issues and, in doing so, produced one of the most valuable contributions to political thought.

 This letter by "Philadelphiensis" (from the *Antifederalist*, 1788) plays on fears that a U.S. president would be even more powerful and dangerous than George III had been.

A **negative** means the power to stop legislation—a veto.

... the president is a king to all intents and purposes, and at the same time one of the most dangerous kind too—an elective king, the commander-in-chief of a standing army, etc. and to add, that he has a **negative** over the proceedings of both branches of the legislature: and to complete his uncontrolled sway, he is neither restrained nor assisted by a privy council, which is a novelty in government. I challenge the politicians of the whole continent to find in any period of history a monarch more absolute.

Speaking at the Massachusetts convention, Patrick Henry launched one of the most powerful attacks on the new Constitution. He began by questioning the basis of its popular authority.

This refers to a unitary or non-confederate government.

Have they said, "We the States"? Have they made a proposal of a compact between states? If they had, this would be a confederation. It is otherwise most clearly **a consolidated government.** The question turns, sir, on that poor little thing—the expression, "We, the people," instead of "the states" of America. I need not make much pains to show that the principles of this system are extremely pernicious, impolitic, and dangerous.

Patrick Henry (1736–99) was the revolutionary statesman from Virginia who opposed ratification of the Constitution and put forward the Bill of Rights as a safeguard of individual and states' rights.

PAPER INTO PRACTICE

George Washington was a clear choice as the first president of the United States.

Early in 1789, states began electing officials for the House of Representatives and the Senate. Both houses convened in New York in April 1789. In 1800, the federal government was moved to Washington, D.C., a specially built capital city between Maryland and Virginia.

Voters in each state directly elected Representatives and Senators. The president, however, was indirectly elected: the states voted for members of an electoral college, which then chose the president. The first president of the United States was George Washington, with John Adams as his vice-president. After a triumphant journey from Virginia to New York, Washington set to work establishing the executive branch of government.

Meanwhile, Congress was filling in the gaps left by the Constitution. It created an attorney general (the chief law officer who represented the government in the law courts) and other federal posts. The Judiciary Act of 1789 set up a judicial structure of thirteen federal courts, three courts of appeal, and a Supreme Court.

Several states had refused to ratify the Constitution without the promise of a bill of rights. James Madison drew up twelve key rights and proposed them as constitutional amendments. By 1791, ten of these rights had been ratified by the necessary three-quarters of the states. The Bill of Rights limits the powers of the federal government to those outlined in the Constitution. It also guarantees certain fundamental rights, such as freedom of speech, religion, and assembly, and the right to bear arms.

The American Revolution was now complete. In the space of fewer than thirty years, the thirteen colonies had found they had more in common with each other than with Britain, and had bound themselves together in a unique republican union. Neither the Americans nor anyone else predicted that the creation of the United States of America would alter the course of world history forever.

In the late eighteenth century, New York City was already a cosmopolitan center of business and enterprise.

PRESIDENT WASHINGTON

In many ways George Washington was the ideal choice as the first U.S. president. Not wanting the president to become a new kind of king, he took great care to stick closely to the letter of the Constitution. At the same time, his personal lifestyle gave the office respect and dignity. He lived in a Manhattan mansion, traveled in a grand coach, and employed almost two dozen servants. A good administrator, Washington wanted the United States to be governed by the most able people, whatever their viewpoint. He was disappointed, therefore, when political parties emerged in the 1790s. He retired to his Virginia home in 1797.

George Washington in retirement, talking with African-American workers on his country estate

 The First Amendment to the Constitution combined several rights previously contained in state bills of rights. The Second Amendment, accepted without a murmur at the time, is controversial today.

> I. Congress shall make no law respecting an **establishment of religion,** or prohibiting the free exercise thereof; or abridging the freedom of speech, or of the press; or the right of the people peaceably to assemble, and to petition the government for **a redress of grievances.** II. A well regulated militia, being necessary to the security of a free state, the right of the people to keep and bear arms, shall not be infringed.

This did not stop states from having an established church.

This means dealing with their complaints.

In Federalist Paper No. 67, Alexander Hamilton complains bitterly about the way the powers proposed for the president in the Constitution had been grossly misrepresented by Antifederalists.

Scrupled means hesitated.

Apprehensions are worries.

This refers to the perceived similarity between the president and a monarch.

An executive officer, here the president.

Prerogatives are powers.

> Calculating upon the aversion of the people to monarchy, [writers against the constitution]... have endeavored to enlist all their jealousies and **apprehensions** in opposition to the intended President of the United States... To establish the **pretended affinity,** they have not **scrupled** to draw resources even from the regions of fiction. The authorities of a **magistrate,** in few instances greater, in some instances less, than those of a governor of New York, have been magnified into more than royal **prerogatives.**

CHAPTER 5

THE IMPACT OF THE REVOLUTION
PARTIES AND POWER

The changes of 1765–91 had an impact on every aspect of American life. First, the tie with Britain was cut, and the United States was established. Second, an enduring framework of government was set up. Third, the new country was free to expand westward and tap its vast economic potential (see map). Nevertheless, two important developments remained before the new system could operate effectively: political parties and a means of interpreting the Constitution.

The Constitution made no mention of political parties, which were commonly associated with corruption and self-interest. Nevertheless, parties emerged in the 1790s. The Democratic Republicans formed around Thomas Jefferson, who stood for the rights of the states, individual liberty, and agriculture. The

Thomas Jefferson (1743–1826), third president of the United States and leader of the Democratic Republicans

THE WESTWARD EXPANSION OF THE UNITED STATES

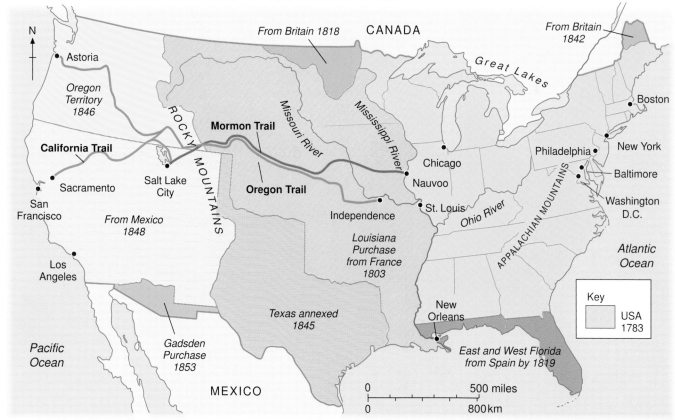

conservative Federalists, inspired by Hamilton and John Adams and supported by the wealthy classes, wished to build up the power of the national (federal) government. By 1796, parties operating in Congress organized the Jefferson-Adams presidential election, which Adams won. From this time forward, the party system has been a key feature of American politics.

Although the Constitution was the basis of government, its wording needed practical interpretation. For example, what did Article I, Section 8 (1), mean when it gave Congress taxation and spending powers for the "general welfare of the United States"?

Working on the premise that the Constitution was the highest law of the land, the right of interpretation went to the federal courts. This principle was brilliantly set out in Chief Justice John Marshall's ruling in the Marbury v. Madison case (1803). This development gave the Supreme Court a great deal of power over American life. For example, the Fourteenth Amendment (1868) tried to protect African-Americans by granting civil rights to "all persons born or naturalized in the United States." The 1875 Civil Rights Act attempted to put this into practice. However, in 1883, the Supreme Court declared the act invalid. This undermined the Fourteenth Amendment, and African-Americans were not guaranteed full civil rights until the twentieth century.

1875 CIVIL RIGHTS ACT

One hundred years after the Declaration of Independence, Congress passed a Civil Rights Act to give all citizens—whatever their "nativity [birth], race, color, or persuasion, religious or political—the right to use inns, public transport, theatres and places of public amusement." This was an attempt to end discrimination against nonwhites. However, the Supreme Court ruled that the act was not based on the Fourteenth Amendment and was therefore unconstitutional, because it sought to protect rights that were social, not civil.

 An important principle of American political life, the right of the federal courts to interpret the Constitution (judicial review), was established by Chief Justice John Marshall. His famous ruling in the *Marbury v. Madison* case made the Supreme Court the "umpire of the Constitution."

Expound means to explain.

It is emphatically the province and duty of the judicial department to say what the law is. Those who apply the rule to particular cases must of necessity **expound** and interpret that rule. If two laws conflict with each other, the courts must decide on the operation of each. So if a law be in opposition to the constitution; if both the law and the constitution apply to a particular case... The court must determine which of these conflicting rules governs the case. That is the very essence of the judicial duty.

John Marshall (1755–1835)

WHOSE REVOLUTION?

The states allowed only adult males to vote in federal elections. In every state except Vermont, the franchise (right to vote) was further limited by wealth or property qualifications. In 1789, only about 25 percent of adult males had the vote; women and nonwhites were excluded.

The Constitution's first three words—"We, the people"— seemed to promise equality for all Americans. It took more than two centuries for this promise to be fulfilled. White men benefited first. Property qualifications for voters were largely gone by 1840; ten years later, all American adult white males had the right to vote.

Ironically, the Revolution set back female suffrage. By 1807, the states that had formerly allowed women to vote in local elections had withdrawn that right. It was restored in Kentucky in 1834. In 1869, the territory of Wyoming (a state as of 1889) granted full female suffrage. Other states followed over the next fifty years, until the Nineteenth Amendment (1919) declared that voting was not to be restricted on account of gender. However, full civil rights did not come with enfranchisement. Only in the late twentieth century were American women beginning to enjoy the civil rights implied by the Revolution.

The Revolution's greatest failing was sidestepping the issue of slavery. Because the economy of the southern states was based on slave labor, they would not have joined a union in which slavery was illegal. The issue was therefore swept under the carpet until it was settled by the Civil War (1861–5). Even after the abolition of slavery in 1865, discrimination plagued many areas of American life, especially in the South, until the Civil Rights movement of the second half of the twentieth century.

For American Indians, the Revolution spelled disaster. It opened up American Indian homelands in the West to pioneers. Sporadic fighting on the frontier culminated in defeat for American Indians in the Indian Wars of 1865–80. Although granted American citizenship in 1924, they continued for years to suffer from discrimination.

For women and nonwhite Americans, therefore, the Revolution fell short of its own high expectations. Nonetheless, it

Women voters in New Jersey, around 1800. Shortly afterward, women's right to vote was removed—only to be restored later in the century.

The Union army captures Atlanta (1864) on the way to victory in the Civil War (1861–5).

THE LEAGUE OF THE GREAT PEACE

Ironically, democracy and federalism had been practiced in North America long before the white man arrived. They were key features of the League of the Great Peace, formed in the sixteenth century or earlier by five Iroquois nations. The League respected the rights of each nation (tribe) and gave all people a say in government. Women were highly respected and had the right to appoint and remove chiefs. White men studied the League's customs, which influenced the form of the U.S. government.

Iroquois villages on a mid–seventeenth-century map

gave Americans a vocabulary of rights, liberty, and equality that would eventually guide them toward a truly democratic future.

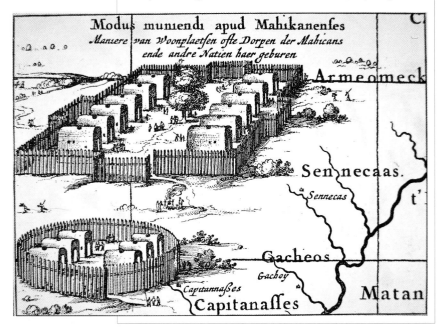

This excerpt comes from an address written by Jupiter Harmon, an early African-American poet, to his fellow African-Americans in 1787. The writing gives some insight into the disappointment African-Americans felt at being excluded from the benefits of the Revolution.

Late means recent.

That liberty is a great thing we may know from our own feelings, and we may likewise judge so from the conduct of the white people in the late war. How much money has been spent and how many lives have been lost to defend their liberty? I must say that I have hoped that God would open their eyes, when they were so much engaged for liberty, to think of the state of the poor blacks, and to pity us.

This means so busy trying for.

VIVE LA LIBERTÉ...!

France took part in most stages of the American Revolution. Its war with Britain had led to the Stamp Act and the colonial tax revolt. The ideas of the European Enlightenment, many coming from France, inspired Americans in their quest for natural rights. And, when war came, French forces played a crucial role in American victory.

Meanwhile, American ideas and influences swept back across the Atlantic Ocean. Wealthier members of the French middle class, preoccupied with a romantic notion of America as a haven of liberty inhabited by noble farmers, adorned their mansions with engravings of American scenes. "Republic" and "liberty" became the words of the moment.

On a political level, French participation in the American Revolution brought the French monarchy to a crisis. The royal government spent more than twice its annual income helping the Americans defeat the British. Most of the money was raised not in taxation but in loans it could not hope to repay. The result was financial disaster.

The French Revolution began in 1789. The citizens of Paris, many poor and starving, stormed the Bastille, a royal fortress and prison. The revolution spread throughout the country. An elected national assembly (like Congress or a parliament) began reforming the country's old-fashioned government and traditions. In 1792, France removed King Louis XVI from power and became a republic, like the United States.

Several leaders of the French Revolution drew their inspiration from the United States. If Americans had improved their lot through revolution, why not the French? The Marquis of Lafayette, who had fought with Washington (after whom he named his eldest son), was just such an idealist.

The Marquis of Lafayette (1757–1834), the French revolutionary leader who learned his republican principles in the United States, where he fought with George Washington

French revolutionaries install a Liberty Tree of their own (about 1789).

The declaration of rights he presented to the French National Assembly was unashamedly based upon the Declaration of Independence. Later, horrified by revolutionary excesses, Lafayette fled the country.

As Lafayette discovered, the two revolutions shared the same vocabulary, but little else. The American Revolution was about national independence and focused on a common enemy—the British. France's revolution began with the disintegration of a regime and developed into a chaotic power struggle between classes.

AMERICAN REACTIONS

In 1789, Americans reacted with delight to the news that the French had followed their example and risen up against their king. Four years later, the leadership of the revolution passed into the hands of radicals who executed Louis XVI and instituted a bloody "Reign of Terror." Some Americans, including Washington, recoiled in horror at this assault on religion, property, and authority. Others, headed by Jefferson, condemned French violence but continued to support what they believed was a fight for freedom.

The aristocratic Vicomtesse de Fars-Fausselandry remembers (right) how passionately she and her friends had supported the American Revolution. They did not believe its principles ran contrary to their own privileged position.

The American cause seemed our own; we were proud of their victories, we cried at their defeats, we tore down bulletins and read them in out houses. None of us reflected on the danger that the New World could give to the old.

Like many Americans, Thomas Paine welcomed the outbreak of the French Revolution. In his preface to *The Rights of Man* (1791–2), he hoped the revolutionary principles would spread to England. But events in France became too hot even for Paine. In 1794, he was arrested in France and released only because he was an American citizen.

This British cartoon of Thomas Paine reflects the widespread disillusionment with revolutionary principles that followed the French Revolution's descent into carnage by 1793.

The cause of the French people is that of all Europe, or rather of the whole world; but the governments of all those countries are by no means favorable to it... There ought not now to exist any doubt that the peoples of France, England, and America, enlightened and enlightening each other, shall henceforth be able, not merely to give the world an example of good government, but by their united influence enforce its practice.

THE POSTWAR WORLD

The immediate impact of the French Revolution was great because it promised so much to so many. It became the pattern for other violent revolutions—from the uprising against the Spaniards in Argentina (1816) to the Russian Revolution in St. Petersburg in 1917.

The long-term impact of the American Revolution was more subtle and more enduring. It taught through example, not force. It gave the world the belief that nations have the right to determine their own future. This concept lay at the heart of the Fourteen Points that President Wilson offered as the basis for a peace settlement after World War I.

The legacy of the American Revolution for the world's great colonial powers was obvious.

During the nineteenth and twentieth centuries, Britain eventually granted all of its colonies their independence. Most other imperial powers did the same.

The impact of the Constitution and its style of government has also been considerable. Written constitutions are now common throughout the world. Many countries, including Canada (1841), Australia (1901), and Germany (1949), have adopted a form of federalism. The rule of law, checks and balances, and the separation of powers are widely recognized as essential to democratic government.

Perhaps the most powerful of all the legacies of the American Revolution has been its concept of individual freedom. It is not a government-led freedom from hunger or poverty, for example. Rather, it is the freedom to speak, worship, assemble, publish, and make money. It is this, more than anything else, that continues to draw millions of people across the oceans to the extraordinary place that is the United States of America.

Welcome to a new world: Italian immigrants arriving at Ellis Island, New York, about 1905

In January 1918, President Woodrow Wilson presented Congress with his Fourteen Points for world peace (right). The principle of national self-determination was featured in many of them.

Program for the Peace of the World
By PRESIDENT WILSON January 8, 1918

I. Open covenants of peace, openly arrived at, after which there shall be no private international understandings of any kind, but diplomacy shall proceed always frankly and in the public view.

II. Absolute freedom of navigation upon the seas, outside territorial waters, alike in peace and in war, except as the seas may be closed in whole or in part by international action for the enforcement of international covenants.

III. The removal, so far as possible, of all economic barriers and the establishment of an equality of trade conditions among all the nations consenting to the peace and associating themselves for its maintenance.

IV. Adequate guarantees given and taken that national armaments will reduce to the lowest point consistent with domestic safety.

V. Free, open-minded, and absolutely impartial adjustment of all colonial claims, based upon a strict observance of the principle that in determining all such questions of sovereignty the interests of the population concerned must have equal weight with the equitable claims of the government whose title is to be determined.

VI. The evacuation of all Russian territory and such a settlement of all questions affecting Russia as will secure the best and freest coöperation of the other nations of the world in obtaining for her an unhampered and unembarrassed opportunity for the independent determination of her own political development and national policy, and assure her of a sincere welcome into the society of free nations under institutions of her own choosing; and, more than a welcome, assistance also of every kind that she may need and may herself desire. The treatment accorded Russia by her sister nations in the months to come will be the acid test of their goodwill, of their comprehension of her needs as distinguished from their own interests, and of their intelligent and unselfish sympathy.

VII. Belgium, the whole world will agree, must be evacuated and restored, without any attempt to limit the sovereignty which she enjoys in common with all other free nations. No other single act will serve as this will serve to restore confidence among the nations in the law which they have themselves set and determined for the government of their relations with one

another. Without this healing act the whole structure and validity of international law is forever impaired.

VIII. All French territory should be freed and the invaded portions restored, and the wrong done to France by Prussia in 1871 in the matter of Alsace-Lorraine, which has unsettled the peace of the world for nearly fifty years, should be righted, in order that peace may once more be made secure in the interest of all.

IX. A readjustment of the frontiers of Italy should be effected along clearly recognizable lines of nationality.

X. The people of Austria-Hungary, whose place among the nations we wish to see safeguarded and assured, should be accorded the freest opportunity of autonomous development.

XI. Rumania, Serbia and Montenegro should be evacuated; occupied territories restored; Serbia accorded free and secure access to the sea; and the relations of the several Balkan States to one another determined by friendly counsel along historically established lines of allegiance and nationality; and international guarantees of the political and economic independence and territorial integrity of the several Balkan States should be entered into.

XII. The Turkish portions of the present Ottoman Empire should be assured a secure sovereignty, but the other nationalities which are now under Turkish rule should be assured an undoubted security of life and an absolutely unmolested opportunity of autonomous development, and the Dardanelles should be permanently opened as a free passage to the ships and commerce of all nations under international guarantees.

XIII. An independent Polish State should be erected which should include the territories inhabited by indisputably Polish populations, which should be assured a free and secure access to the sea, and whose political and economic independence and territorial integrity should be guaranteed by international covenant.

XIV. A general association of nations must be formed under specific covenants for the purpose of affording mutual guarantees of political independence and territorial integrity to great and small States alike.

5. [We want] A free, open-minded, and absolutely impartial adjustment of all colonial claims... [in which] the interests of the populations concerned must have equal weight...

10. The peoples of Austria-Hungary... should be accorded the freest opportunity of autonomous development.

12. The Turkish portions of the present Ottoman empire should be assured a secure sovereignty, but the other nationalities... should be assured an absolutely unmolested opportunity of autonomous development.

A European empire that collapsed in 1918.

Autonomous means independent.

A European–Middle-Eastern empire that collapsed in 1918.

This means free from interference.

In March 1947, President Harry S. Truman outlined a doctrine that, for the first time, pledged practical support for the principles of the American Revolution in other countries.

President Harry S. Truman (1884–1973)

At the present moment in world history nearly every nation must choose between alternative ways of life... One way... is based upon the will of the majority, and is distinguished by free institutions, representative government, free elections, guarantees of individual liberty, freedom of speech and religion, and freedom from political oppression.

The second way... is based upon the will of a minority forcibly imposed upon the majority. It relies upon terror and oppression... and the suppression of personal freedoms.

I believe that it must be the policy of the United States to support free peoples... primarily through economic and financial aid.

GLOSSARY

Admiralty The British government department responsible for the Royal Navy.

Antifederalists Americans who campaigned against ratification of the Constitution. They believed it gave the president too much power and undermined the independence of the states.

Archbishop of Canterbury The appointed head of the episcopal Church of England.

Bill of Rights A legally binding declaration of people's civil liberties or rights. The Bill of Rights includes the first ten amendments to the Constitution (1791).

boycott A widespread refusal to participate in or buy something. Leading up to the Revolution, Americans frequently boycotted British goods.

cash crop A crop, such as tobacco, that is sold for money rather than personal use.

Charles I The king of England (reigned 1642–9) who fought a civil war, lost, and was executed. For the next eleven years, Britain was a republic.

checks and balances A way of limiting the power of different branches of government by dividing powers and duties among them.

commissioner A government official given a specific task.

confederation A loose alliance of states in which supreme authority is retained by the states and not in a central government.

Congress A large meeting or assembly of delegates from several states. The name was chosen for the legislative branch of the United States.

constitution The laws and conventions by which a country is governed.

Continental Congress The congress of all the American colonies (later states).

delegates Emissaries from the states to a congress. Unlike representatives, who were charged with deciding matters for themselves, delegates could fulfill only the wishes and instructions of those who had sent them.

democracy A form of government, famously defined by U.S. president Abraham Lincoln as "government of the people, by the people, and for the people."

dissenters Protestants who rejected the Church of England.

East India Company The powerful British company that had a monopoly of trade with India and the Far East.

English Civil War The war (1642–5) fought between Charles I and Parliament over religion and parliamentary rights.

Enlightenment An eighteenth-century intellectual movement that attacked all practices, especially religious and political ones, that could not be justified by reason.

executive The part of the government, headed by the president, that is responsible for executing (carrying out) laws. This means running the day-to-day government, including maintaining law and order, managing the economy, commanding the military, and conducting foreign affairs.

federalism A system that divides government between a central authority and localities, giving substantial powers to each.

Federalists The Americans who campaigned for ratification of the Constitution.

garrison Soldiers responsible for defending a town or fortress.

Glorious Revolution The British parliament's removal of King James II (James VII of Scotland), replacing him with the joint rule of Queen Mary II and King William III (1688–9). It marked the final triumph of the parliament over the monarch.

judiciary The branch of government, consisting of courts and judges, concerned with interpreting and enforcing the law.

legislature The branch of government concerned with making laws.

Liberty Tree The tree (or pole) before which the Sons of Liberty met and committed themselves to the cause of liberty. The first was an elm tree in Boston. Liberty Trees soon became symbols of the American cause.

Loyalists Americans who opposed the break with Britain. Also known as "Tories."

Members of Parliament (MPs) Members of the British House of Commons.

mercenaries Hired soldiers prepared to join any army as long as they are paid.

militia Local volunteer military forces.

natural law Fundamental law that comes from "nature"—it is not

man-made.

Navigation Acts Laws that protected Britain's trade by stipulating that it had to pass through home ports and be carried in its own ships.

New England The northeastern colonies that were originally settled by Puritan colonists.

New World A European name for the Americas. Europe and the Middle East were known as the Old World.

nonimportation The American campaign to refuse any goods imported from Britain.

ordinance A law passed by the Second Continental Congress.

Parliament The British representative assembly made up of the elected House of Commons and the non-elected House of Lords. The Commons represent mainly the wealthy, while the Lords is made up of nobles.

patriots Americans who resisted the efforts of the British government to tax the colonies and eventually led the colonies into war.

prime minister The chief minister in the British government. Although appointed by the crown, he or she has to have the support of a majority of MPs.

proclamation A royal decree.

Puritan Someone who wished to "purify" the Church of England of its Roman Catholic features, such as bishops. More generally, "puritan" came to mean a strict (and often intolerant) Protestant.

Quaker A member of a Protestant religious group known as the Friends of Truth (later the Religious Society of Friends). Rejecting formal services and professional priests, they believed each individual was guided by an "inner light." The nickname "Quaker" arose because the group's British founder, George Fox, told a judge to quake at the name of the Lord.

quartering Forcing civilians to host and support troops.

radical Someone who calls for total change, plucking up the existing order by the roots.

ratify To accept officially. The Constitution had to be ratified by nine of the thirteen states before it could become law.

representative A person who, by making his or her own choices and judgments, reflects the views of those who have sent him or her. Members of Congress are representatives rather than delegates.

Republic A state without a monarch.

Republican government Government through the people's representatives rather than direct democracy.

revenue Government income.

search warrant A document that gives permission for a search of private property.

self-determination The right of a nation to decide for itself by whom and how it should be governed.

separation of powers The division of government power and duties among the executive, legislative, and judiciary branches. It was a fundamental principle of the Constitution.

standing army An army that remains intact in peacetime. The British distrust of standing armies (which they associated with European tyranny) was shared in the American colonies.

Sons of Liberty A group of American radicals, led by Samuel Adams and Patrick Henry, founded in 1765 to oppose the Stamp Act.

tariff A duty charged on imports.

tyranny A government that acts in its own interest rather than that of the people it governs.

virtual representation The idea that Americans, although they did not elect their own MPs to the House of Commons, were "virtually" represented there in the same way as British people who did not have the vote.

Whig The more liberal of the two British political parties in the eighteenth century.